Egypt under the Pharaohs

Endpapers Carved relief from an Egyptian tomb
showing scenes of mummification

LIFE IN ANCIENT LANDS
Edited by Edward Bacon

Egypt under the Pharaohs

Barbara Sewell

Evans Brothers Limited London

This book was designed and produced by George Rainbird Ltd
44 Edgware Road, London w2,
for Evans Brothers Limited,
Montague House, Russell Square, London wc1.

The text was filmset in Great Britain by
Oliver Burridge Filmsetting Ltd, Crawley.
The book was printed and bound in Yugoslavia.

237 35080 7

CONTENTS

	Foreword, by the Editor	7
	Introduction	9
One	The land and its resources	13
Two	Death and the after-life	31
Three	The Old Kingdom	45
Four	The Middle Kingdom	59
Five	The New Kingdom	63
Six	Society	79
Seven	Domestic life	83
Eight	Writing and literature	95
Nine	Morality and ethics	107
Ten	Law and justice	109
Eleven	Science	112
Twelve	Arts and crafts	118
Thirteen	Music and musicians	137
	Bibliography	140
	Acknowledgements	141
	Index	142

COLOUR PLATES

1	Two shabti statuettes	17
2	Vintage scene	18
3	Male offering-bringers	18
4	Garden scene	35
5	Pet cat under chair	35
6	Papyrus columns at Saqqara	36
7	The goddess Isis	53
8	Osiris	54
9	Queen Tetisheri	71
10	The Step Pyramid at Saqqara	72
11	Fowling scene	97
12	The second coffin of Tutankhamūn	98-9
13	Tutankhamūn's fan	100
14	Casket from the tomb of Tutankhamūn	100
15	Seated scribe	133
16	The weighing of the heart	134-5
17	Egyptian pottery	136

FOREWORD

The world as we know it is a man-made world. Hardly any part of the habitable globe is unaffected by man's activity; even some of the parts which are uninhabitable were made so by man. And man himself is very largely a man-made creature; his habits, his thoughts, his memory, his aspirations are the modified sum of his ancestors' experiences.

All men are brothers, say the missionary and the idealist. True, but there is more to it than that: all men, living and dead, since the beginning of time, are our brothers; and all history is family history. The Magdalenian artist of 17,000 years ago who decorated the caves of Lascaux with bulls and horses, the Cretan who applauded the bull-leapers, the Egyptian who drew funny hippopotamuses on pieces of stone, the boy Inca who triumphed in the initiation tests, the Etruscans who delighted so frankly in wine, women and song – these are as real to us, as near to us and as sustaining to us as, at any rate, some of those who live in our own street, village, town. Or they can be.

Aristotle said that the object of poetry was pleasure. And when he used these words, he doubtless used them in the widest possible sense: poetry, to include the full range of man's creative imagination; pleasure, to encompass everything from the baby's first chuckle to the philosopher's cry of delight at apprehending a new facet of truth. Education and the pursuit of knowledge have two objectives: pleasure and power. And of these the greater is pleasure: power is transitory, pleasure is permanent.

If these books enable anyone to pass an examination, to secure a job or to dominate a competitor or friend, they will have served a purpose of a sort. Their main objective, however, is to increase the sum of human pleasure, to enlarge the circle of friendship, love and knowledge, and to present a picture of life.

No other civilization has yet lasted as long as the Egyptian. The Great Pyramids were more remote in time from Cleopatra than are the builders of Stonehenge from the modern Londoner. And throughout that unbroken 3,000 years or more, the Egyptian culture is extraordinarily consistent. The products of Cheops, of the Ramessids, even of the Greek Ptolemies, are all immediately recognizable as Egyptian. There is something at first chilling and depressing about this excessive and hieratic civilization.

Before the British Museum started rearranging its ground floor galleries, there were three parallel galleries by which the visitor could reach the further stairs leading to the upper floors. One of these was Greek, and the dominant colour was creamy white; the second was Assyrian, and grey; and the third was Egyptian, and its stones were black and that extraordinary brawn-like porphyry. The measure of the Greek galleries was idealised man; that of the Assyrian, the man of military might; that of the Egyptian, the all-powerful priest. The impact of Assyrian and Egyptian was alike chilling and overwhelming, but the effortless and supremely self-confident Egyptian austerity was the most daunting of all.

But things, thank Heaven, are not always what they seem. The Greeks were by no means as ideal and beautiful as they appear; the Assyrians, surprisingly, had a taste for charm, beauty and tenderness; and the Egyptians, in the massive shadow of their monolithic conservatism, had also, as will appear in these pages, a capacity for humour, wit and family affection which is utterly delightful.

EDWARD BACON

INTRODUCTION

The ancient Egyptians loved life. Whatever else is obscure in the records surviving from this most ancient of the great civilizations this fact is abundantly clear. In the words of a leading authority "they were gay, light-hearted, luxurious and inclined to ostentation; prone to self-indulgence and not proof against sensual temptations . . . kind, charitable, courteous, perhaps less callous to pain than other nations of antiquity. Honesty and incorruptibility were not among their strong points, but . . . they were at least able to perceive the ideal standard if they did not attain to it."* They were "gifted but not deep; their aversion to dull brooding, and their love of all that is artistic and pleasurable in life are characteristics [which] help to endear them to their modern votaries". It is their intense enjoyment of living and of life in all its forms that partly explains the fascination they hold for us, evoking as it does an immediate emotional response to their essential humanity which can be universally understood, and which is so different from the remoteness experienced when contemplating other ancient peoples. On the other hand, the incomprehensible mystery surrounding so much of the ideas and motives expressed in their art and literature and in the forms of their monuments poses by contrast a never-ending puzzle which only adds to the curiosity and interest which they arouse.

This ancient culture must be approached across the intervening eras of Greece and Rome and all that followed subsequently until our own time, and our interpretation of it tends to be coloured by an outlook based on a heritage of reasoning completely alien to that of a primitive culture which had come to an end before the foundations of our own had fairly been laid. Nevertheless the nature of the Egyptian climate has preserved so many objects – in particular those personal and everyday utensils and possessions which reveal more than anything else the character of a people – that the Egyptians can be brought intimately close in human terms, and it is possible to have personal knowledge of individuals by name, with all their quirks and foibles, and to trace generations of the same family.

The decipherment of the hieroglyphic script, virtually unknown about a century and a half ago, has played a most important part in our getting to know the Egyptians through their writings and inscriptions, and is indeed the basis of any reliable information about them. It is largely the extraordinary advance made in the study of the ancient Egyptian language since the end of the nineteenth century that has transformed the science of Egyptology from the romantic and fanciful interpretations of nineteenth century explorers and dilettani into the sober and factual analyses now accessible

* Sir Alan Gardiner: *Ethics and Morality*, p. 484

bearing on every aspect of the life and culture of Egypt. In conjunction with the great strides made in scientific archaeology, it is possible to form a picture of ancient Egypt and its people with a fair amount of accuracy and authenticity, in spite of the tantalizing lacunae which still exist in so many instances but which may suddenly be filled by a fortuitous turn of the spade or the elucidation of some hitherto obscure meaning in a text or inscription.

The Egyptians' technical achievements demonstrate a degree of skill and sophistication that was unique in their contemporary world. In contemplating them it is sometimes difficult to remember that the peak of this amazing civilization was reached before the end of the second millennium B.C., and some eight or nine hundred years before the zenith of the Roman Empire. The story of ancient Egypt was practically over, and much of it had become legendary, by the time St Augustine came to England.

Much of the following account of the life and works of the Egyptians may give the impression of sombre preoccupation with death, and of confused and illogical thought and reasoning. The Egyptians seem illogical because they were in fact a primitive race: abstract thought was alien to them, and the primitive mind demands a concrete image to express itself. The readiest example of this is the multitude of gods and goddesses with their anthropomorphic and animal forms, which were often combined. Egypt had emerged from the neolithic age by about the beginning of the fourth millennium B.C., and a thousand years later the people of the Nile Valley had developed an integrated culture and a relatively advanced civilization that was eventually to become the inspiration of the Greek genius, which in its turn was to evolve its own incomparable culture.

The history of ancient Egypt covers a period of some 3,000 years from the time when historical records are available until the conquest of Egypt by Alexander the Great in 332 B.C., after which Egypt was ruled by Greek (Ptolemaic) kings and later by Roman emperors.

As yet no very clear picture can be formed of what happened in Egypt prior to the beginning of the dynastic period, and although a corner of the veil can be lifted here and there, the story is largely guesswork and only really begins with the unification in c. 3100 B.C. of the northern and southern parts of the country, called by the Egyptians the Two Lands. The southern part consists of Upper and Middle Egypt, from the First Cataract at Aswan to the apex of the Delta; the Delta region itself constitutes Lower Egypt. When one ruler reigned over the Two Lands he was called the King of Upper and Lower Egypt.

The historical period can be roughly divided into five main parts: the Early Dynastic Period (consisting of the first two Dynasties of kings, c. 3100–c. 2686 B.C.); the Old Kingdom (Third to Sixth Dynasty, c. 2686–c. 2181 B.C.); the Middle Kingdom (mid-Eleventh to Twelfth Dynasty, c. 2050–c. 1786 B.C.); the New Kingdom, sometimes called the Empire (Eighteenth to Twentieth Dynasty, c. 1567–c. 1085 B.C.); and the Late Period (Twenty-first to Thirtieth Dynasty, c. 1085–c. 343 B.C.). It was during the New Kingdom that Egypt attained her zenith as the leading power of the ancient world, with an empire which extended from Nubia in the south to the Euphrates in the north-east.

Besides these five broad historical divisions two Intermediate Periods are recognized,

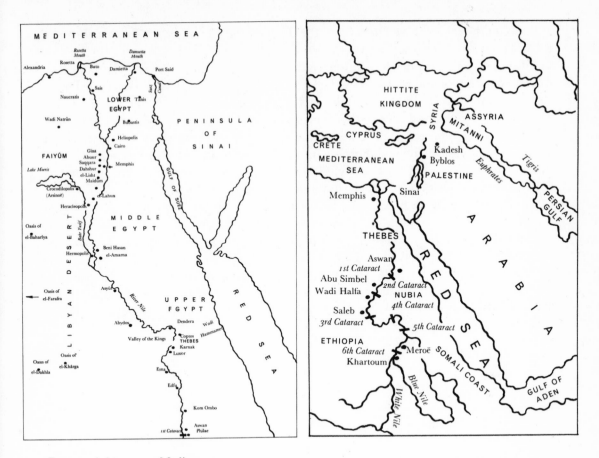

Egypt and the eastern Mediterranean

one occurring between the Old and Middle Kingdoms, when the central government for various social and political reasons collapsed and gave rise to a time of confusion and rival claims for control; the other between the Middle and New Kingdoms when, owing to a decline in the dynastic power at the end of the Twelfth Dynasty, foreign immigrants of Asiatic origin who had been infiltrating and settling in the Delta region took advantage of the disrupted state of the country to seize and dominate a large part of the Delta and Middle Egypt. At the same time the south was retained under the control of various native provincial princes, the strongest of whom were at Thebes (the modern Luxor), and who, after some years of alternate uprising against the foreign rulers and peaceful coexistence with them, finally grew strong enough to expel them altogether from Egypt and to reunite the country once more under a single strong rule, to usher in the New Kingdom when Thebes became established as one of the greatest capitals in antiquity and as the religious and political centre of the Egyptian Empire. Long after its decline in the sixth century B.C. the fame of this fabulous city lingered on, and even today it is the focus for tourists where the impressive ruins demonstrate by their extent and grandeur the glory that was described by Homer as "hundred-gated Thebes".

11

Between the downfall of Thebes and the dawn of the Christian era Egypt's fortunes fluctuated between prosperity under native rulers, which included dynasties of Nubian and Libyan kings, and periods of domination by the Assyrians who, in 664 B.C., were driven out of Egypt and replaced by the last native Egyptian dynasty. This hailed from Sais, a town in the Delta, and under it Egypt regained much of her former glory. During this Saite period there was a renaissance of the Old Kingdom art and fashion which was even reflected in dress and hair styles, the past being taken as a model for a conscious nationalistic revival. Foreign immigrants were attracted to Egypt as a centre of culture and learning, notably the Greeks who were allowed to found a colony at Naucratis in the Delta from which they carried on their trade.

The Saite kings were finally conquered in 525 B.C. by the Persian Cambyses, who founded a dynasty of Persian rulers in Egypt. After some years of rebellions and uprisings against foreign overlords, in which the Egyptians were aided by the Greeks, Alexander the Great arrived as the conqueror of Egypt and founded the city of Alexandria. When, after his death, Alexander's empire was partitioned, one of his generals, Ptolemy Lagus, was appointed to govern Egypt, and he became the founder of the Ptolemaic dynasty of Greek kings which lasted until Egypt became a province of Rome in 30 B.C.

Chapter One

THE LAND AND ITS RESOURCES

Herodotus's saying that Egypt is the gift of the Nile is true. The valley of the Nile itself constitutes the land of Egypt which extended in the pharaonic period from the Mediterranean in the north to the First Cataract at Aswan in the south. Beyond this lay the vast indeterminate region of Nubia and Ethiopia through which flowed the Nile from its source in the heart of Africa just above the Equator. This fabulous river, some 4,000 miles long, forcing its way through a network of watercourses and torrents across the Sudan, Ethiopia and Nubia, progresses by six cataracts of rocky barriers forming islands and islets as far as the First Cataract where it emerges into the desert bringing with it fertilizing sandy clay deposits to enable life to flourish in the midst of the desert wastes along a narrow strip of land, seldom more than eighteen miles in width, on its 750-mile journey to the sea. Just north of Cairo it branches out into two main arms intersected by innumerable natural and artificial canals across the Delta plain; in ancient times it emerged into three great lakes, but these have since largely silted up so that it now reaches the sea by way of the Rosetta and Damietta mouths. It is flanked on either side of its total length from Aswan to Cairo by the Libyan and Sahara deserts to the west, and, to the east, by the Arabian Desert.

The Egyptians described their land as "The Black" and "The Red", to distinguish between the habitable fertile region fed by the Nile and the inhospitable desert; the sea which was their northern boundary, and led to the outside world of the "vile foreigner", they called the "Great Green". More precisely the name for the southern part of the country, that is, Upper and Middle Egypt, was written with a flowering reed plant which grew in abundance in the Nile Valley but which is unidentifiable today; the name of the northern, Delta region, or Lower Egypt, was written with a clump of papyrus plant which grew in tall, extensive thickets in the marshy swamps of that region and, indeed, over large areas of the rest of the country as well, both wild and in cultivated fields. The reed and papyrus symbols assumed an almost heraldic significance to denote the territorial and political divisions of the land, and were extensively developed as artistic motifs connected with royalty, notably in the combined design to be seen carved on the sides of royal thrones, the two intertwined plants symbolizing the unity of the two parts of the country under one ruler. The manifold use of papyrus no doubt increased its importance as a favourite motif in architecture and in the minor arts, and gave rise to innumerable variations of stylistic design.

The plant was extensively used from the very earliest times for all kinds of purposes, the chief of which included supporting columns for early temples and shrines; these columns, made of bundles of papyrus stalks bound together, were later to be copied in stone, with the papyrus flower at the top becoming the capital. Light rowing boats and,

Middle Kingdom tomb carving showing the construction of light boats from papyrus

more generally, compact floats were made by stringing together three bundles of the stems tied narrowly at the ends. Rafts were also made by lashing together bundles of the stems which were kept flat by sticks fitted across them, resembling the simple floats made of maize or dura stalks still occasionally seen in Egypt today. Papyrus was also used for making sails, and strips of it were woven into mats. The split stems were used for making boxes and sandals, examples of which have been found in Tutankhamūn's tomb and in others; and also for rope and cordage. Even the base of the stems was not wasted since it was eaten as a great delicacy, especially when cooked. Its most famous use was, of course, in the manufacture by special processing, the secret of which is lost, into writing material from which our own word for paper is derived. This all-purpose plant had its aesthetic value as well, and, with its decorative umbels, was used for ceremonial bouquets fit to be presented to the gods in their temples and to the dead in their tombs; and also as floral decorations for banqueting halls. By virtue of its perennial green it was used in hieroglyphic writing as the sign for "green", and to denote meanings of "joy" and "youth". This supremely typical Egyptian plant is no longer to be seen growing in Egypt, although it flourishes still in Israel and Sicily where it was transplanted in ancient times. Its disappearance from Egypt is due largely to the silting up of the marshes which were once the scene of so much animated bird and animal life, and the happy hunting ground of the ancient Egyptian sportsman.

Already in neolithic times, about 5000–4000 B.C. when primitive agriculture was practised in the Nile Valley and a definite stone age culture already existed, the Delta had silted up to form a natural protective barrier between the lands beyond the Great Green and Egypt. By 4000 B.C. the wadis of the north and the oases of the western desert had been established. The oases, now grouped together into the three great oases of Khârga-Dâkhla, el-Farâfra and el-Baharîya, and Siwa, were the remains of where the Nile used to flow in early geological times and formed part of the pharaonic kingdom. They were then much more verdant than they are now, and were noted for their vineyards whence came many notable wines to the royal court. It is difficult now to

Above left. The first cataract of the Nile. *Left*. King Sesostris of the Twelfth
Dynasty wearing the white crown of Upper Egypt (right) and the red crown
of Lower Egypt; from a carved lintel. The unification symbols, papyrus
and reed, appear on the side of his throne, and above is the winged sun-disc

15

imagine this when one contemplates the present wilderness, although ruins of temples still standing in the oases bear witness to their ancient fertility. From the Wadi Natrûn in the north came the natron used in the process of mummification and for ritual and other purposes. Of the date palm groves that no doubt once flourished in the oases nothing now remains. Groves of date palms are nowadays planted round villages not only to provide welcome shade but for economic purposes, and taxes are levied on them; in ancient times taxes were levied on fruit-trees, and, very likely, on palm groves which also provided timber for roofs and for door lintels, these forms also being later copied in stone. On the site of ancient Memphis there is now a grove of date palms surrounding the modern village there, in the midst of which stands a somewhat forlorn-looking but magnificent alabaster sphinx representing one of the pharaohs of the New Kingdom period. A few stone column bases are all that remains of the great temple of Ptah, the god of Memphis, which once stood there and which was founded by Menes, the traditional first king of the First Dynasty (c. 3100 B.C.) in the city which became the capital of Egypt, and remained the spiritual if not always the actual capital throughout Egyptian history.

It was Nature's gift of the Nile with its annual inundation which enabled civilization in Egypt to gain the lead over its contemporaries by providing a natural object lesson in the basic principles of agriculture. The river begins to rise about the middle of June bringing rich deposits of mud from Abyssinia in its wake, and gradually floods the land on either side of its banks until it reaches its height in September when it falls rapidly so that by April or May it is at its lowest. It leaves behind a rich layer of fertile black mud ready for the sowing of crops which in the rich soil and in practically unending sunshine yield abundant harvests with very little trouble. In a country with no rainfall the Nile, besides maintaining underground reservoirs and creating heavy nocturnal dews, is the only source of irrigation. It is small wonder that from the earliest times the Nile and its control was – as it still is today – the keystone of the economy and the political focus of the country. It was doubtless the recognition of this vital fact by some enlightened tribal chieftain in prehistoric times which brought about the situation which is inferred from the emergence of Menes (about 3100 B.C.) as the great unifier of the northern and southern parts of the country and the first king of a united Egypt. Whoever controlled the Nile waters and organized their distribution had the monopoly of power in his hands, and it can be demonstrated over and over again throughout Egyptian history (and this applies as much today as then) that when there was a strong centralized government to ensure this Egypt flourished; but famine and hard times resulted whenever the central authority, for whatever reason, weakened or disintegrated. Since the very life of the community depended on the annual inundation of the Nile, it is obvious that the river and all it meant was the basis and centre of the Egyptians' thought and development and dictated much of their beliefs and pattern of behaviour. It is perhaps not too much to say that the whole structure of the culture of pharaonic Egypt sprang from the Nile. The Egyptians orientated themselves by it: the south was the river's source, east and west were either side of the river whichever way it flowed. On the rare occasions when it rained, the Egyptians called it a "heavenly inundation".

Needless to say the Nile, or rather the dynamic essence which caused it to rise, was deified, and was personified by the god Hapy. The river itself was a separate deity.

Plate 1. Two shabti statuettes, one in blue faience (Dyn. XXI), the other in painted limestone (Dyn. XVIII-XIX)

If Nature was generous in providing suitable conditions for the neolithic farmer to sow his seed in the alluvial mud-flats left by the receding Nile flood and wait for the hot sun to ripen it, a great deal of hard work was called for to control the abundant water supply and to make the best use of it. In summer the lower ground was flooded completely and only isolated mounds appeared like islets in the midst of the sea. Under the centralized control of the unified rule of the early dynasties of kings, a co-ordinated system of dykes was constructed to direct the water into organized channels. The river constantly changed the face of the land by creating mounds, depressions and swamps formed by its continually fluctuating branches. In order to bring under cultivation as much land as possible large reclamation schemes were put in hand by levelling the land, at the same time preserving areas of marshland for the rearing of cattle, and for hunting and fishing. Simple reservoir constructions were made to conserve and distribute the flood water at the proper times; an intricate network of canals was dug and maintained, and when the Nile receded in the autumn then came the time for sowing crops. Whereas nowadays it is possible by means of high dams to irrigate all through the year, it was then only possible once a year at the time of the flood.

There were indeed artificial means of irrigating orchards and gardens from nearby rectangular basins or pools built to receive a regular supply of water through some natural branch of the river, or by specially made canals. The fields and gardens were laid out in square plots formed by narrow irrigation channels surrounding them which were fed by the primitive and extremely laborious method of filling two pots on either end of a yoke with water and pouring their contents into the channels. All that was needed was unlimited human labour and time; and of these there were plenty in ancient Egypt. It was some centuries before an improvement on this method took place when in the New Kingdom the *shadûf* was introduced. This consists of a horizontal beam fixed across two pillars of wood or mud-daubed rushes, about five feet high, set up about a yard apart. Over the horizontal beam pivots a long slender pole, to one end of which is suspended a bucket, while at the other a large lump of clay acts as a counterpoise. Standing on a platform at the water's edge, a man pulls down the bucket and fills it with water while the counterpoise lifts it waist high; he then empties the bucket into the irrigation trough which conducts the water into the channels to flow over the land. By this means water can be raised to a height of six feet or more. A long time elapsed before this method changed with the introduction, possibly by the Achaemenides in classical times, of the water wheel drawn by an ox. Both the *shadûf* and the water wheel are still familiar sights in the Egyptian countryside today.

Indeed, to get the best idea of what the ancient Egyptian landscape looked like in the cultivated areas around the villages it is only necessary to ride through the fields around Luxor, or any other country district for that matter, preferably on donkey-back (as this form of transport has not changed), to see the same symmetrical patchwork of square plots of land, irrigated by channels, with men pulling up water by the *shadûf* – almost an exact replica of similar scenes painted by the ancient Egyptians in their tombs. The nature of some of the crops has changed; but many of the birds and other animals in the fields can be recognized as direct descendants of those depicted in the painted scenes. The water wheel too can still be seen, drawn nowadays by a camel or a buffalo.

Plate 2. Vintage scene from the tomb of an unknown nobleman of the Eighteenth Dynasty

Plate 3. Male offering-bringers carrying ducks and eggs, lotus flowers, and a sheaf of papyrus plants. From a private tomb at Thebes (Dyn. XVIII)

Alabaster sphinx at Memphis, representing a pharaoh of the New Kingdom

Some of the most spectacular reclamation work and irrigation schemes were undertaken in the region of the Faiyûm depression on the west side of the Nile in Middle Egypt where a long narrow lake fed by a branch of the Nile, the Baḥr Yûsuf, still preserves this area as one of the most beautiful and fertile parts of Egypt, a veritable oasis of green in the surrounding Libyan desert. In ancient times this internal lake was so much larger that it was called a sea. Today it is one of the most carefully cultivated agricultural areas of Egypt, but then it swarmed with fish and fowl and other wild life in the coverts surrounding its many ponds and backwaters. As well as being a favourite royal hunting ground, it was the seat of a busy fishing industry providing fresh and salt fish on a large scale for the towns. Crocodiles found an ideal home there, and it is not difficult to understand why the chief deity worshipped in the region was Sobek, the crocodile god, who continued to hold sway when the Greeks ruled over Egypt in the second century B.C. They named the chief city of the region Crocodilopolis where Sobek was faithfully worshipped by the Greek settlers, although it eventually became the city of Arsinoë, the wife of one of the Ptolemies.

Fortunately there was no shortage of manpower in ancient Egypt, for the construction and maintenance of the dykes and canals demanded continual attention. The

A gardener watering with a *shadûf*; detail of a wall-painting in a Nineteenth-Dynasty tomb at Thebes

work was carried out by manual labour with the aid of a hoe and a basket into which was flung the mud hacked up in making the canals and channels and later to be used in building up the dykes. The State controlled the work on the dykes and, because these were so vital to the prosperity of the whole community, corvées of workers were levied from all over Egypt at the proper seasons to repair and construct them. It seems that everyone was liable to be called on for this service, and it is only to be expected that those who could afford to, and had enough serfs to call upon, sent deputies whenever possible. This is probably the origin of those quantities of attractively fashioned shabti, or servant statuettes, which from the Middle Kingdom onwards were buried in the tombs (plate 1). These statues, appropriately mummiform in shape, hold in their hands crossed over the breast a hoe, with a basket slung on the back. The inscription which often adorns them reflects their origin, and says: "O this shabti! If So-and-So (the tomb owner) is required for corvée duties in the Hereafter, say thou: here am I." As time went on, instead of a single shabti to deputise for any unpleasant tasks which the deceased might be called upon to perform in the Hereafter, hundreds of these statuettes were placed in the tombs according to the owner's status and means. They attained truly exquisite forms when destined to serve the nobility or kings and queens.

Egypt has always been an agricultural country and neither the crops nor the climate have altered appreciably since the days of the pharaohs. Then as now the sun blazed forth from an almost cloudless sky to give equable temperatures varying between 100°F. (38°C.) in summer and 65°F. (18°C.) in winter. Rainfall is practically unknown save in Lower Egypt when it occurs sometimes during the winter months. Directly the sun goes down, however, there is a sharp fall in temperature and the heavy nocturnal dews render the nights chilly and often cold with thick fog patches before dawn. The winds which the deserts attract from the Mediterranean in the north temper a climate which, by its proximity to tropical Africa, would otherwise be unbearable, and the funerary stelae show that the Egyptians recognized this saving grace by mentioning as one of the desirable accompaniments to a happy eternity a wish to breathe the sweet air of the north wind. The cold nights following the heat of the day, during which the Egyptians rested and slept then as now, gave rise to the kind of ailments to be expected, and the ancient dwellers of the Nile Valley suffered in the same way as their modern counterparts from colds and rheumatism. Many prescriptions in the medical treatises are for these complaints, including the magico-medical incantation by which colds are bidden to "be off, cold son of a cold", and one wonders whether these treatments were any less efficacious than those of today.

The well-known dryness of the Egyptian climate (which has preserved so much more material evidence for the archaeologist than has survived in other more humid parts of the world), in conjunction with the moisturizing properties of the Nile, produced a near-perfect climate suitable on the one hand for brick-making and cooking in the open air by the sun's rays, and on the other for the growth of a large variety of crops and fruit. As against this, the main disadvantages of the climate, apart from the cold nights, were the dust storms which blew in from the desert in the spring and caused as much inconvenience in olden times as they do today, to which were added the pestilential stagnant pools left by the flood at the end of the summer when the heat was at its worst.

In their carefully irrigated fields the Egyptians grew cereals, emmer and barley, flax, from which linen was made, and the ubiquitous papyrus. All these are still grown today in somewhat different varieties, with the exception of papyrus, but to them must be added rice, maize, a kind of millet called sorghum, and sugar-cane and cotton, the two last forming the main agricultural industries of present-day Egypt. It is interesting to see the modern peasant or fellah chewing at the root of a long piece of sugar-cane unconsciously imitating his forebears who enjoyed eating the root of the papyrus stalk.

The Egyptians were great market-gardeners, and planted their orchards and gardens close to their houses and above the dykes to escape the flood waters. Garden produce included an appetizing array of vegetables: beans, lentils, chick-peas, cucumbers, onions, lettuces and melons; beans and lentils remain the staple diet of the less well-to-do in Egypt, forming the foundation of the typical Arabic dish, *fūl*. The luscious bowls of fruit with which the tables are loaded in scenes of banquets and funeral repasts show that grapes, figs, dates, citrus fruits and pomegranates were plentiful. The variety of fruit has increased since then, although all these old native products are still seen in present-day Egypt.

One of the basic necessities of life was oil, which was used not only for food in large quantities, and as fuel for lamps, but also in toilet and medical preparations. Many

Herdsmen feeding oryxes; painting in the tomb of Khnumhotep. Middle Kingdom

kinds of oils were known, of which the chief were castor oil and ben oil from the moringa tree. The olive tree does not seem to have been cultivated in Egypt until New Kingdom times, and even then olive oil was still largely imported; but from very early times, at least as early as the Old Kingdom, it appears in the offering-lists in tombs and temples, and was doubtless one of the commodities imported from Palestine and Syria. Oil also appears in lists of payment due to workers employed on public works such as pyramid and tomb building, together with other wages in kind: linen, sandals, vegetables and cereals.

In the cultivated parts of the country trees grew in isolated clumps or were planted in groves, and in addition to the dôm and date palms, the tamarisk, persea and Christ's thorn were to be found; and, the commonest trees of all, the acacia and sycomore fig beneath whose shade the Egyptian and his wife are so often depicted at ease enjoying the cool of the sweet north breezes in their garden, and drinking a draught of water from the pool which was built in the garden of everyone who owned a villa of any pretensions (plate 4).

Beyond the area of cultivation and the papyrus swamps and thickets stretched the desert – a complete contrast to the smiling fertility and order of the arable land. Yet at this period it was not the desolate waste of rocks, dried up wadis and sand dunes that it is today. The desert had a life of its own, and was known and exploited by a totally different type from the prosperous folk of the farming communities, and the luxury-loving and sophisticated town-dwellers of the Nile Valley. In the swamps and marsh-lands grazed herds of cattle and other domesticated animals such as ibexes, sheep, goats and pigs, tended by herdsmen who led a semi-nomadic life.

The desert was full of wild life, and the oryx, antelope, ibex, gazelle and wild goat offered excellent game for hunting, always a favourite sport among the nobility; while bigger game, such as lions, wild bulls, and ostriches, befitting royalty, was reserved rather more exclusively for the pharaoh and his court (plate 13). At night the bark of the hyena was heard and wolf-like dogs emerged to prowl around the rocky wilderness of the western desert where the dead lay buried in their rock tombs and pyramids. This animal still exists and prowls about his ancient haunts as if still protecting the dead. It embodied Anubis, the god of the necropolis and of embalmers, and guide and protector of the mummy. It appears in most tombs either painted on the walls or in statue form with its lithe body, long pointed ears and muzzle, and bushy tail. Its black coat does not represent the colour of mourning and death, but the black-coloured resin used on the body in the embalming process and therefore associated with preservation of life and resurrection. Other more sinister inhabitants lurked in the desert: the cobra, the deadly horned viper, scorpions and locusts which brought dread to the heart and gave rise to a vast collection of magical spells and prayers to recite, and amulets to wear, to ward off their potential danger. More attractive was the small wild life which abounded in the desert and which appears so charmingly depicted in many of the hunting scenes. Living close to nature as they did, the Egyptians were accurate and sympathetic observers and, with the freer hand in depicting animal life than was allowed in representing humans and gods owing to the hallowed conventions which surrounded them, the artists happily caught in a spontaneous style the swift passage of a hare or fox, the protective gesture of a gazelle or antelope in shielding its young from the flying arrows of the hunters, and the panic flight of these small creatures before the charge of the king in his chariot as he transfixes a herd of lions single-handed, followed by a crowd of

Tutankhamūn hunting lions; scene on one side of a painted wooden box found in his tomb

admiring courtiers in chariots and on foot. This convention of the king, who is depicted larger than anyone else, slaying his prey, whether animal or human, has its roots in the earliest representations of his conquering might on the predynastic slate palettes. The same motif can be followed right through to the latest period, with at times more elaborate and elegant details, but remaining basically the same in design. It represents the unshakable belief in pharaoh's might and domination inherent in his person and does not necessarily imply a display of megalomania.

The papyrus swamps teemed with life, and the wild cats, genets, ichneumons and other denizens of the marshes were all included in scenes where the tomb-owner was shown in a favourite attitude harpooning a hippopotamus, or bringing down the flying duck and other fowl with his throwstick (plate 11). Nor were the dwellers in the water forgotten: the Nile teemed with fish, as it still does and very largely of the same species, and, apart from fishing for sport, humbler folk fished by different methods for industrial purposes. Fish dried in the sun and salted formed an important part of the diet of the ordinary people, but was taboo for kings and priests and offerings to the dead. Most fish from the Nile were edible and included carp, the Nile perch (a particularly succulent fish), *Mormyrus oxyrhynchus* (the sharp-snouted Nile fish), and mullet from whose compressed eggs was made a kind of proletarian caviar.

The Egyptians' fondness for flowers is at once apparent in every representation of daily and ceremonial life, in their houses, gardens, temples and palaces, and in personal adornment and jewellery. No feast or entertainment, religious or secular, for the living or the dead was complete without them. Most of the species are uncertain from a botanical point of view with one or two exceptions, but cornflowers, daisies and lilies are recognizable. The flower which typifies ancient Egypt even more than the papyrus

Harpooning hippopotamuses; sculptured scene from the tomb of Mereruka at Saqqara. Old Kingdom

25

Left. Tutankhamūn as a child, emerging from the blue lotus flower. *Right.* Guests at a banquet wearing cones of scented wax on their heads; painted scene from the New Kingdom tomb of Two Sculptors at Thebes

is the lotus or water-lily of which there were two varieties, one blue with denticulated petals, and one white with smooth pointed petals. They were found wherever there were calm waterways and pools, their flowers opening and closing at morning and evening. Here was a heaven-sent symbol after the Egyptians' own hearts which they were not slow to seize upon to incorporate in their creation myths. In one of these the lotus personifies the sun-god springing from the heart of a lotus flower resting on the primordial waters of chaos. At evening the flower closed, and in the morning it opened, just as the sun sets to rise again the next day. The king, who was the physical son of Rē the sun-god, exemplified this idea, and in Tutankhamūn's tomb was found a model of the king as a beautiful child emerging from the blue lotus flower. Without any feeling of contradiction, the blue lotus was at the same time the emblem of the god Nefertum of Memphis who was the lord of perfumes, the blue lotus having a delicate and delicious scent; it had the same significance for the Egyptians as the rose has for England. Guests at banquets were handed blue lotus flowers which they held delicately to their noses breathing not only the delicious perfume for pleasure, but symbolically contemplating their own hope of rebirth after death. This favourite of all flowers was further used architecturally in the carved capitals of temple columns imitating clusters of the lotus buds and, together with the papyrus flower capitals, formed one of the most character-istic features of Egyptian architecture (plate 6).

It is to be expected that an oriental people should set great store by perfumes and exotic scents which they extracted from pressed flowers. The most common, however, were scented oils which were used extensively for anointing the body and hair. At festivals and social gatherings guests are shown with a cone of scented wax on their heads, and as the festivities advanced and the heat increased, the perfumed mixture melted and ran down in refreshing rivulets over head and shoulders at the expense, however, of their pure white linen garments which it stained. Incense was an essential part of the ritual both in the temple and funeral ceremonies, and for this the most precious and exotic perfumes were sought from the distant coasts of the Red Sea where gum and resin-bearing trees grew. These regions, known to the Egyptians as the land of Punt, were the objective of many expeditions sent out by the pharaohs, led by their most important ministers, to acquire by means of barter with the natives luxuries unobtainable in Egypt, among which were included the highly-prized incense trees for transplanting at home. Small laboratories for manufacturing perfumes and unguents were attached to the temples, and one of these rooms still exists in the temple of Edfu, its walls covered with inscriptions describing the recipes for their preparation. It is not possible to reconstruct these ancient exotic scents owing to difficulties in the translation of the ingredients, but it seems that the most subtle of them took six months to prepare.

From the evidence of the tomb paintings and the hieroglyphs there appear to have been more than twenty-nine different kinds of birds in Egypt, and most of these are drawn and painted and carved with extraordinary skill and acute observation by the Egyptian artists and sculptors (plate 11). No marsh scene was complete without them, and most of these birds were identified with some god or goddess and associated with one or other town, locality, or aspect of life. The most notable are the birds of prey: the falcon, identified with the god Horus, the son of Osiris and incarnated in the reigning monarch; and the vulture who incorporated two important goddesses, Nekhbet, and Mut, the spouse of the god Amūn. From the time of the Middle Kingdom, Amūn grew in importance, originating as the local god of Thebes from whence the founders of the Middle Kingdom dynasties of kings arose. He became the supreme state god and assimilated the attributes of all the other local and national gods, including Osiris, so that Mut was also the mother of the reigning Horus, in other words, the king. This is reflected in the feathered vulture headdress worn by the king's Chief Great Wife, the queen (plate 9).

The marshes and waterways harboured numerous varieties of wading and web-footed birds, including herons of various kinds, duck and geese. Pied kingfishers and sandmartins were also common. Field birds seem familiar to us because they are identical in most cases with those seen today in the Egyptian countryside: crows, rooks, hoopoes, pigeons, swallows and that most typical of field birds, the white heron. Sparrows then as now were regarded by a farming community as pests, and were used as a hieroglyph to denote anything small, mean or bad.

The Egyptians experimented in taming the different varieties of wild horned cattle – bulls, antelopes, ibexes, gazelles – and wild goats and barbary sheep which roamed the desert edge and the Delta marshes in prehistoric and early historic times. During the Middle Kingdom domestication was mainly confined to animals such as pigs, sheep, and cattle which were more suited to confinement in large herds capable of being cared for by one or two shepherds.

Cows and goats were used for milking, and oxen for dragging the plough; and at harvest time oxen, sheep and goats were driven on to the threshing floor to tread out the grain. Ibexes and oryxes were also reared, and the herdsmen – tough, half-savage marsh-dwellers – seem to have been devoted to their flocks, going to great lengths to protect them from danger, feeding them by hand, and carrying the young calves and kids when moving their herds across streams and fords too swift and deep for the young ones.

The little African donkey was as familiar a sight in Egypt then as it is today; from time immemorial it has been the patient servant of man, and apart from its use as a pack animal it helped to carry in the harvest.

Every well-to-do nobleman in Egypt possessed a vineyard on his estate to supply him not only with dessert grapes, but with the wine of which he was so fond that it was considered no breach of good manners for him or his womenfolk at parties to indulge to excess, sometimes with disastrous results, as can be seen in the details of some of the banqueting scenes faithfully portrayed by the all-observant Egyptian artist. But there

Herdsmen with cattle; sculptured scene from the tomb of Ti at Saqqara. Old Kingdom

was also a flourishing industry in the production of wine from many renowned State vineyards and from temple estates. The best quality wines came from the fertile oases, and a particularly choice vintage came from the Libyan border of the Delta region. In the New Kingdom Ramesses II had his residence in the Delta and spent much time and energy in developing and inspecting a vineyard on his royal domain, which became the most famous of its day and which was called "The Upholder of Egypt". It is tempting to see in this a double-edged allusion to himself as pharaoh and to the properties of the wine. From the vineyard, in addition to some five hundred others, he states that he donated to the temples of Amūn wines without number from the southern and northern oases and from Upper Egypt. In Lower Egypt, referring to "The Upholder of Egypt", he says he multiplied the vineyards into "hundreds and thousands" – a conventionally hyperbolic statement characteristic of all royal utterances, and one that remains an oriental trait.

Vintage scenes are portrayed in great detail in the tombs, where the process from gathering the fruit to the final "bottling" in large pottery jars can be closely followed

Woman vomiting at a banquet

(plate 2). The grapes, from which red and white wines were made, were crushed by treading, the residue of the pulp after the first extraction being placed in a cloth or bag and tightly twisted to extract the remainder. The juice was then poured into the jars and left to ferment. When fermentation had almost ceased, the jars were stoppered with a wad of vine leaves or rushes and completely covered over with a mud or clay capsule, moulded over the mouth and neck of the jar. If fermentation was still going on at this stage, a small hole was drilled in the neck of the jar or in the stopper to provide an escape for the small remainder of carbon dioxide, and the hole finally stopped with a wisp of straw or sealed with clay. The vintner's seal was then impressed upon the clay, and the jar marked with the year of the reigning king together with the name of the district and the vineyard, and a note as to the quality of the wine: "three", or "eight times good". The wine was left to mature, sometimes for many years. The Egyptians treated their wine with respect, and the connoisseur was able to judge from the marking the relative maturity and quality of the wine which had come, for instance, from the vineyard of "The Food of Egypt", or from the estates "on the western branch of the river", or from Pelusium: "Star of Horus in the height of Heaven". The name of the Chief Overseer of the Vineyard was always included on the label and no doubt bore its own cachet.

Wine jar from the tomb of Tutankhamūn. The hieratic inscription gives the year and name of the vintage

Chapter Two

DEATH AND THE AFTER-LIFE

One of the first things that comes to mind when thinking of the ancient Egyptians is the elaborate preparations they made for their tombs and what may seem to us their bizarre burial practices, particularly the preservation of the dead body by mummification. This sprang not from a morbid preoccupation with death but from sheer love of life as they knew it on earth, and the desire to perpetuate it after death. The need to possess a thing, or the essence of some quality, required a concrete image to bring it into existence. The word "Maat", which is translated as "truth" in the sense of "what is right", the "right order", represented the established order of the universe as it was conceived to be; the gods in their places, fulfilling their proper functions for the benefit of mankind, the forces of Nature under control and life in general proceeding on its way in the proper manner. The way to ensure this was to create an exact image of the ideal, to bring it into being, and to imbue it with life by means of appropriate magical formulae: the likeness of a man or woman in a portrait-statue, generally idealistically portrayed in the prime of life, caused that person to exist permanently. The same applied to representations of food and drink, clothes and possessions, servants, animals and one's own house – the tomb itself. This was built as like the owner's earthly habitation as possible, and other necessities of life were faithfully depicted on the walls.

The elaborate burials of the kings in their pyramids and rock-cut tombs ensured not only a prolongation of the king's own existence, but a guarantee of "Maat", which it was the king's function to maintain for the whole land and its population. The scenes sculpted and painted on the walls of the royal tombs were of a magical or religious nature, designed to overcome the obstructive forces of the Underworld which, according to the mythology connected with the king's destiny after death, strove to prevent his entry into the company of gods and deified ancestors. The different concepts of the fate which awaited him (some of which originated in prehistoric times) were eventually fused, or rather confused, into a palimpsest of notions and pictorial representations which, even in the light of accompanying written texts (which do little to illuminate them), are frankly bewildering in their meaning for us and, one suspects, for the Egyptians themselves after they had become stereotyped. The fact that they were sanctified by age-old custom was reason enough for the conservative Egyptians never to discard them; the Egyptians simply superimposed new ideas and beliefs as they evolved in order to retain the efficacy of representational truth to achieve their ends.

On the other hand, owners of private tombs, while arrogating to themselves the essential magico-religious aspirations of royalty for the after-life which they hoped to share according to their worldly status and position, depicted also scenes of earthly life and occupations and thus present us with invaluable documentary evidence of almost

Ti and his wife inspect cattle on their estates while scribes (lower register) make the inventory; sculptured scene from the tomb of Ti at Saqqara. Old Kingdom

every activity and pursuit of their daily lives. Many of these scenes, it is thought, were originally copied from those which adorned the walls of the palaces of the living kings which, being built almost entirely of mud-brick and wood, have not survived. The material used for the construction of their everlasting homes had to be more durable and their tombs were either built of stone or cut into the rocks of the desert hills. The sands of centuries did the rest by protecting them to a large extent until excavators of modern times brought them to light and exposed them to the ravages of the weather and the rather more potent destruction of vandals and tomb robbers.

In pursuing the quest for life by making permanent representations of the needs and luxuries which they hoped to retain beyond the grave, the arts of architecture, sculpture, carving and painting were developed almost unconsciously in an effort to achieve a practical end. It was done not "for art's sake" but as a means of achieving a concrete end:

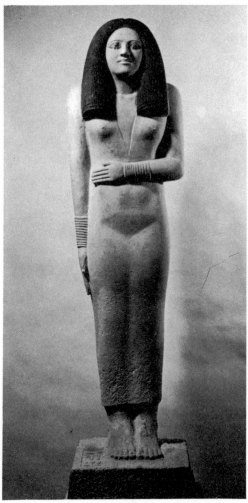

Limestone portrait statues, nearly life-size, of Sepa and Neset (Dyn. III). Sepa holds the staff and baton carried by all men of position in the Old Kingdom

the continuation of life. The Egyptian word for a portrait-sculptor literally means "one who makes to live". The effort to create in visual form a true image of the desired object to "make it live" was the original inspiration for an artistic development of the highest order; while the existing remains of temples and pyramids bear witness, even in their ruined state, to the architectural achievements of the ancient Egyptians. Their artists set out to gain the practical object of eternal life as it is known on earth; in this they manifestly failed, but in doing so they succeeded through their innate talent and sensitive observation of nature and the world around them in achieving something they did not originally intend. It is obvious that they took pleasure in expressing themselves in their artistic work, though since much of it was done to rule and convention, this was incidental. If we tend to assess their work from a purely aesthetic viewpoint, we are entitled to do so and can gain a great deal of pleasure; but much will be lost and misunderstood if we fail to keep in mind the true motive behind it. It is significant that works of Egyptian art, even masterpieces of which there are many, never bear the artist's name, and in only a few instances are the names of individual artists and sculptors known or any appreciation of their work recorded.

The Egyptians' ideas of what happened after death are probably unique among ancient peoples, for they believed that it was a continuation of the world as they knew it, and they could not imagine any kind of life which did not depend on the body and its physical needs. They thought that the gods as well as men in order to survive needed air to breathe, food and drink, clothes and houses. But let them speak for themselves; the most common prayer carved at the entrance to every tomb gives us an idea of what they considered necessary for survival after death, and thus they besought the living:

> O all you who pass by this tomb, may you make an offering of bread and beer, oxen and
> geese, cloth and linen, incense and myrrh, and all things good and pure on which a god
> lives, for the *ka* of So-and-So . . .

This prayer was generally accompanied by a picture of the deceased carved on a stela or stone block, seated at a table loaded with offerings of food and drink with which he regaled himself. Lists of offerings were often added and included bread, beer, oxen, geese, and fine linen, and members of the dead person's family were shown presenting them. These stelae became in time more elaborate and included, as well as suitable prayers and praises of the dead person's qualities, his titles and biographical details.

They could not fail to observe what happened when death occurred to men and beasts, but they believed that by preserving a man's body from decay and putting it in a tomb like the house in which he had lived, supplying food and drink, and surrounding him with his possessions, he would have all that was necessary to subsist in the next world, which was imagined to be an idealized version of life on earth. From the time of the Old Kingdom they learned how to embalm dead bodies, and attempts at mummification continued to be practised with varying degrees of success right up to Greco-Roman times.

While there is little doubt that a dead man's family and descendants would keep up the supplies, which was indeed their duty if they hoped to gain the same benefits for themselves when they died, there was no guarantee that succeeding generations would continue, or even be able to do so. The well-to-do therefore left a large portion of their wealth to priests attached to the cemeteries, or to a nearby temple, to maintain the necessary food-offerings and other ritual offices at regular intervals and on special feast days. This priestly function became hereditary, and there grew up a permanent body of *ka*-priests endowed and specially trained to fulfil these duties.

The precise meaning of the *ka* is not known. There is no parallel in modern thought with this abstract notion, and the nearest translation of it to our understanding seems to be that it represented the "vital force" of life itself, and of the power which creates and sustains life. When a man died it was said that "he went to his *ka*", and lifelike statues of the deceased were placed in the tombs, the implication being that these portrait-like statues contained the vital force of life which was sustained by the victuals offered for their consumption. The gods in the temples likewise needed this nourishment offered daily to their statues in order to sustain their power; and the king who, through

Plate 4. Scene from the tomb of Userhet, a high priest of the Nineteenth Dynasty. With his wife and mother under a sycamore tree he is being offered refreshment by the tree-goddess. The souls of Userhet and his wife, in the form of birds, are poised above the pool, indicated by zigzag strokes, the hieroglyphic sign for water
Plate 5. Pet cat eating fish under the chair of its owner, Nakht, scribe and astronomer

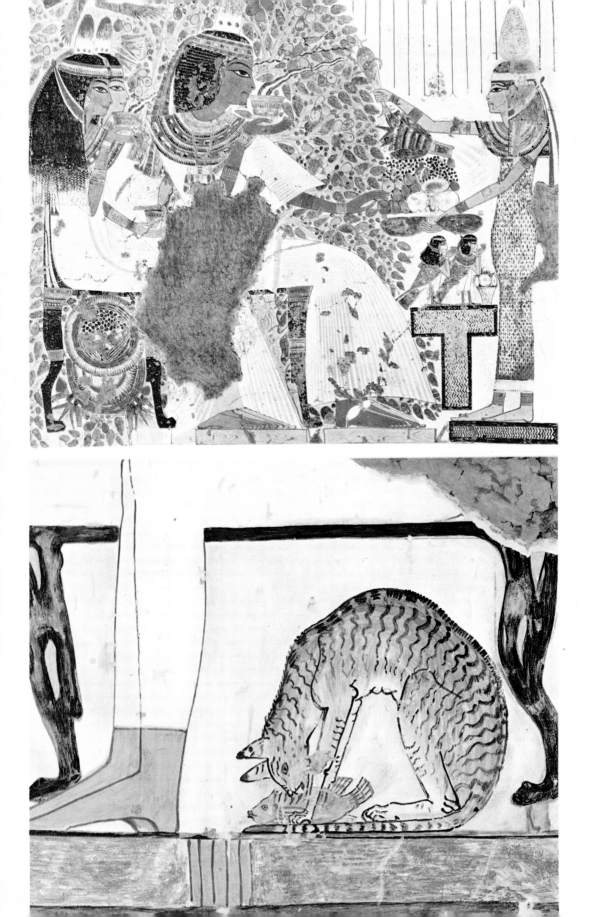

his semi-divine descent, partook of the essence of this universal life-power, performed certain daily rituals in the temples to this end. What of course happened was that the king, who did in fact perform these duties, was represented in the different temples throughout the land by priests acting on his behalf. This daily sustenance enabled the gods to renew their energy and creative force and consequently the continuance of life in general. The idea had its roots in the primitive conception of the sacrifice, in other words the giving of life in return for life.

The burial privileges, originally reserved for the king alone, were assumed in time by everyone who considered he had a claim to them by virtue of his office, or the powers delegated to him by the king, and in the final event by anyone who could afford it. Naturally there came a time when the provisions for keeping up the tomb and its equipment either ran out or were neglected by future generations. Again, this fact must have been all too apparent, and to guard against it the vital necessities were ensured by representations carved and painted in great detail on the tomb walls (plate 3). To these were added the pleasures and pursuits of daily life such as hunting, feasting, and supervising property, with armies of servants in attendance to supply the needs of the deceased as they had done in life. If anything should occur to destroy the body, or if the provisions failed, the *ka*-statue and the pictures remained to take their place. More than physical death an Egyptian feared to "die a second time in the necropolis". If his tomb or his body were destroyed this was indeed the end. It was therefore the supreme revenge to deface or in any way to damage a man's tomb; and there are many instances on the tomb-walls of the faces and names of the owners having been ruthlessly hacked out by some enemy.

The interiors of the best preserved tombs present the liveliest and most colourful aspects, and to spend an hour or so among the painted and decorated tombs of the nobles in, for example, Luxor or Saqqara is to recapture more than a little the busy, gay and above all colourful life of ancient Egypt, particularly when, on emerging once more into the twentieth century, one encounters so many present-day examples of the animals and plants and even physical human types so faithfully depicted by the ancient artists.

Although the tomb, so gaily decorated and containing so many treasured possessions, was intended as a permanent home after death, this did not prevent the formation of ideas about the sort of world the dead inhabited. In characteristic Egyptian fashion, several theories could happily exist side by side without any feeling of contradiction. The afterworld was, according to one of the most general beliefs, a region somewhere in the west, the region of the setting sun, which is why most of the cemeteries are situated in the western desert. The sun-god, Rē, was the supreme deity, and when he rose every morning it may be that this unalterable natural event indicated a renewal of life, a re-birth. It is not surprising in a land like Egypt, where the sun never fails to shine, that it was from early times worshipped as the supreme life-giver. In the development of the sun religion, the king became the son of the sun-god: "Son of Rē" from Old Kingdom times onwards formed part of the king's titulary, and it was thought that when the king died he went to the west to join his father, journeying with him through the hours of darkness to be reborn with him again each morning, thus ensuring continuity of life for his people. It is possible that the pyramids of the early dynastic kings may have symbolized the idea of a "stairway to the sky", a phrase indeed which occurs in some

Plate 6. Engaged columns from one of the buildings in the pyramid complex of Djoser at Saqqara, showing the imitation in stone of the papyrus plant

of the ancient pyramid texts in connection with the king's death.

The assimilation of the king with the sun-god Rē later included Osiris, whose cult seems to have had its origin in the Delta region. One theory is that Osiris came from Byblos with which, from very early times, the Egyptians maintained strong trade relations for the acquisition of coniferous timber for their building and other purposes, and Byblos remained throughout the pharaonic period, if not always a vassal of Egypt, then certainly in the closest relations with her. Many ideas and influences from Mesopotamia must have infiltrated into Egypt from the very beginning as soon as the first sea-going ships were built to undertake the sea journey to the shores of south-east Asia. Be that as it may, Osiris is attested in documents only in the second half of the Fifth Dynasty, and by the end of the Old Kingdom his cult, together with that of Rē, had developed and spread all over Egypt so that Osiris had to be taken into account in connection with the fate of the dead king. According to one version of the Osiris myth, Horus was the son of Osiris who avenged his father's murder by his brother Seth. The living king was identified with Horus, consequently the dead king, his father, became Osiris. With the wave of democratization which swept over Egypt at the end of the Old Kingdom, the dead king's prerogatives of burial rites and his destiny after death were claimed by everybody, and rich and poor alike at death became "Osiris".

The water used in lustration rites for the dead Osiris was partly the reason why

Carving depicting Osiris, on the wall of a chapel at Dendera, placed so as to receive the rays of the sun

Osiris came also to be identified with the Nile and its flood, so becoming integrated with the growth and rotation of the crops; and the promise of resurrection demonstrated by the birth, growth, decay and rebirth of nature suggested an obvious theme for application to the fate of mankind. Hence the aspect of Osiris as a king of the dead, when he is depicted as a dead god in the form of a mummy, and sometimes coloured green by virtue of his association with the crops (plate 8).

Another version of the Osiris legend had such a human appeal that it became the universally popular belief about death and the hereafter among the mass of the people, and no doubt was more readily acceptable than the more esoteric solar beliefs which were based on extremely antiquated doctrines and applied only to the king. In this version, Osiris was murdered by Seth, who mutilated his body and drowned it in the Nile, to be sought throughout the length and breadth of Egypt by his devoted wife, Isis (plate 7), who finally recovered and restored it by revivifying magic, and bandaged it in the form of a mummy. This was something that could be readily understood and with it the promise it held out of resurrection after death in perpetual association with the king.

Osiris became identified with, and sometimes superseded, most of the principal gods of Egypt, and his traditional burial place at Abydos remained always the centre *par excellence* of his cult, and was the scene of annual pilgrimages when the drama of his story was performed by actors wearing appropriate masks, and playing to a set script, traces of which have been found. These "passion plays" were evidently written to a classic formula with cues for speeches, dancing and mime. It would be interesting to know what kind of music accompanied them, but though it is known what kinds of musical instruments the Egyptians played on, nothing in the way of musical notation has survived. Everyone who could afford it had a cenotaph or a commemorative stela erected at Abydos so that his name might dwell in this most sacred part of Egypt.

The aspect of Osiris as a vegetation god symbolizing the rebirth of life in the fields is reflected in a rather charming custom that was carried out at the recession of the Nile flood, when the fields emerged ready for sowing. Little figures of Osiris made of damp clay and mixed with seeds were put in a clay bed and placed in the tombs. When the germinating seed had sprung up the Osiris figure became green as if with renewed life. A number of these withered "corn Osiris" figures have been recovered from private tombs, and are a touching memento of a personal and picturesque demonstration of a common and consolatory belief. Similarly in Egypt today, at certain religious festivals, the descendants of the ancient Egyptians unconsciously perpetuate the tradition of their ancestors by placing germinating lentils in damp cotton.

The private tomb of the Old Kingdom consisted of a burial chamber at the bottom of a vertical shaft which was sealed after burial, and a superstructure above the ground, rectangular in shape with slightly inclined walls. The shape of these tombs resembled the mastabas or stone benches outside Arab houses and this led to their being known as mastaba tombs. A small chapel was added to the eastern side of the mastaba, where food-offerings were placed and rites and ceremonies performed at the time of burial and on certain feast days and anniversaries. The statue of the deceased was walled up in an enclosed corridor called the serdab and was able to communicate with the living world and receive the offerings placed for it through a slit in the dividing wall. In this wall was incorporated the stela on which was carved the figure of the dead man seated at the table and the prayer for offerings to his *ka*. These stelae became more and more elaborate, until they symbolized a doorway to the tomb evidently modelled on the entrance doors to actual dwelling houses. It is on these "false doors" that are found, in addition to the formal prayer for offerings, the names and titles of the deceased and often biographical histories that throw much light on the way in which the land was administered, besides revealing interesting personal details of the lives of individuals. The offering formula had its roots in the early dynastic period; it became stereotyped and was retained in the same form throughout the whole period of Egyptian history.

The chief intention behind it was to ensure that the essential provisions should be forthcoming by virtue of the king's bounty through the agency of certain gods associated with the dead. The gist of the prayer, which is to be seen on practically all tomb stelae and other funerary monuments, is as follows: "A boon which the king gives [to] Osiris, lord of Busiris, the great god, lord of Abydos, that he may give invocation-offerings consisting of bread and beer, oxen and fowl, jars of ointment and clothing, all things good and pure on which a god lives, to the spirit of the revered So-and-So, justified." The epithet "justified", or "true of voice" after the deceased's name is added as an indication that the dead man has been proved innocent before the tribunal of the gods, who assessed his earthly actions and behaviour before judging him worthy to enter the company of gods in the life beyond. This theory of what happened after death, based on one of the ancient myths forming part of the Egyptians' religious beliefs, casts an interesting light on the morality and ethics of the Egyptians, which will be referred to later.

In some cases the statue is shown coming through the false door to receive his offerings and to enjoy once more the sight of the world he had loved so much. A fine example is in the tomb of one Mereruka, a vizier of the Sixth Dynasty. In course of time, the chapel before the serdab became extended into a series of rooms which later filled the whole superstructure of the mastaba, and which contained furniture, stores and other personal possessions, and on the walls of which were represented the scenes of daily life which have been described. The room before the serdab was retained as a mortuary chapel and the inscriptions here were devoted to the lists of offerings and magical texts which were to form a permanent insurance of continuity in the Hereafter.

The burial chamber contained the body of the deceased enclosed in a large wooden coffin, at first rectangular and later mummiform in shape, decorated with hieroglyphic texts of prayers and magical spells. Some anthropoid coffins were decorated with a painted feather design, representing the wings of the goddess Isis in the form of a bird protecting the body of Osiris, with whom the dead were identified (plate 12). As time went on, and burials became more elaborate, two and sometimes three coffins fitting into one another were provided, each heavily decorated inside and out with texts, amuletic symbols and other religious scenes.

In the case of royalty the coffins were enclosed in massive stone sarcophagi, usually very finely carved to represent the façade of the royal palace, and inscribed with texts. By the time of the New Kingdom the coffins were of gold or gilded wood. The unique find of an intact royal burial in the tomb of Tutankhamūn in 1922 demonstrated a royal burial equipment in all its splendour (plate 12). There were three coffins, all

Mereruka emerging from the false door of his tomb at Saqqara. In front is the offering-table on which food and drink were placed

elaborately decorated, the innermost one, containing the Pharaoh's mummy, being of solid gold and weighing 242 lb, and beautifully carved. The sarcophagus was of fine yellow quartzite, although its lid was obviously made separately and possibly hurriedly, as the material used is a rose quartzite and the workmanship is of an inferior kind to the base. The coffins and sarcophagus were enclosed in four gilded wooden shrines, each fitting precisely inside the other, and all adorned with inscriptions and figures of protective deities very finely executed. The outermost shrine, which was inlaid with blue faience, measured at its base 16 feet 6 inches by 11 feet, with a height of 9 feet 9 inches.

The magnificent alabaster sarcophagus of Sety I, which is preserved in the Sir John Soane Museum in London, and whose tomb in the Valley of the Kings is perhaps the largest royal tomb known, is unusual, if not unique, in being mummiform in shape. The sarcophagus and its cover were hollowed out of two single blocks of alabaster and were covered inside and out with finely carved inscriptions and illustrations of mythological scenes connected with the king's journey through the Underworld. These carvings

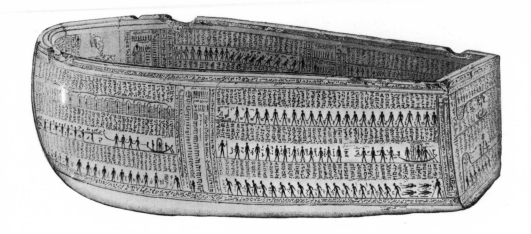

The alabaster sarcophagus of Sety I

were originally filled in with some kind of paint of a vivid bluish-green colour, which, contrasting with the brilliant whiteness of the polished alabaster, must have presented a magnificent sight.

The name "mummy" derives from Arabic *mumya*, a word meaning bitumen or pitch, which passed through late Greek and medieval Latin into most European languages, and was originally believed to be the material used in mummification. Mummification in ancient Egypt was practised from the beginning of the dynastic period until the early Christian era. The first attempts were not very successful, and experiments and improvements were always being tried. The highest standard was reached in the New Kingdom, the remains of many of the most famous pharaohs and other notabilities of that period that have survived being identifiable with their known statues.

The Egyptians themselves left only incomplete accounts of the processes which they employed, and most of what is known about them has been learnt from the Greek historians and travellers, Herodotus and Diodorus, writing at a late date, about 400 and 100 B.C. respectively, so that the method described by them may have changed over the centuries. It is said that in the best and most expensive form of mummification, an incision was made in the side and the contents of the abdomen and thorax removed. The brain was removed by smashing the ethmoid bone in the nose, breaking up the brain with a metal instrument, and then pulling it down through the nostrils with a hook. The body was then treated with natron, and the cavities filled with linen, sawdust and resin, and then anointed with cedar oil. It was finally bandaged in a most intricate way, each limb separately, and gum or molten resin poured over the mummy.

Only the rich could afford this method which is said to have taken seventy days. The

Stoppers from the painted alabaster canopic jars found in the tomb of Tutankhamūn (*top*) and canopic jars of Neskhons, wife of the High Priest of Amūn at Thebes. The stoppers of the canopic jars of Neskhons are carved to represent the heads of the four protective deities, Hapy (ape), Duamutef (jackal), Imsety (human), and Qebhsenuef (falcon)

second, less expensive, way consisted of injecting cedar oil to dissolve the internal organs, and the body was bandaged and wrapped as before; the cheapest method consisted of merely cleaning the body with a purgative and handing it back to the relatives for burial when it was wrapped in a simple shroud. The heart and sometimes the kidneys were left in the body, the intestines, liver and lungs being removed, mummified and wrapped separately and placed in four canopic jars, so called because early antiquaries were reminded by their similarity in shape to an image of Osiris worshipped at Canopus in the Roman period. The stoppers of these jars were carved to represent the heads of the four deities whose function it was to protect these vital organs. Before the Nineteenth Dynasty it was customary to fashion the stoppers in the form of human heads, presumably representing the deceased, like the very fine examples found in the tomb of Tutankhamūn.

Chapter Three

THE OLD KINGDOM

About 17 miles south of Cairo lies a plain, to the east of which flows the Nile. Here, where Upper and Lower Egypt meet, the first king of the First Dynasty, traditionally known as Menes, built a fortress which was known as White Walls. It is generally held that Menes was the king who, about 3100 B.C., finally resolved the struggle which had evidently been waged during the predynastic period between the north and the south by two loose confederations of communities. Little is known of this period, but one or two facts are clear. The leader or "king" of the northern confederation was distinguished by a headdress called the Red Crown of Lower Egypt, while the southern "king" of Upper Egypt wore a white one. These two pieces of headgear (later combined as one crown) remained throughout Egyptian history the royal crown, symbolizing the unification of the two lands under one ruler. It was Menes, the southerner, who finally succeeded in conquering the north and uniting Egypt under his sole authority, and Memphis was the place he rightly chose to found his capital, this being a strategic point from which to control the country.

This great event in Egypt's history is depicted on the famous ceremonial slate palette of King Narmer, who has been identified with Menes, and constitutes one of the earliest historical records in existence. The meaning is clear: Narmer (Menes) on one side of the palette wears the Lower Egyptian red crown and on the reverse is shown wearing the white crown of Upper Egypt. Other symbols of royalty already established at this early date are also shown, and they persisted with unbroken regularity in connection with the kingship throughout the whole of Egyptian history. The Egyptians were a conservative race, for the good reason that the creation of a symbol and its representation automatically imbued it with actuality. The sacred symbols of royalty therefore were essential for the preservation of the king's power. Other symbols and customs were added later, and were duly given a place in pictorial representation, but the old ones were never discarded, even when their original meaning had been superseded or may even have been forgotten.

Memphis then became the first capital of a united Egypt, and remained the spiritual if not always the geographical capital throughout the centuries. Today all that is left of the city of the White Walls are a few scattered ruins surrounded by a palm grove. Nearby is the modern village of Saqqara, where a score of kings and their courtiers were buried from the earliest dynasties onwards, and which remained the site of cemeteries until well into the Greco-Roman period. The huge mastaba tombs of the first two dynasties (c. 3100–2686 B.C.), discovered at Saqqara since the end of the Second World War, point to a culture and technical advance which, despite its archaism and limitations, was sufficiently established to promote the remarkable and

45

The ceremonial slate palette of Narmer. On one side (*right*) he is depicted wearing the Red Crown of Lower Egypt, with his standard-bearers and rows of beheaded enemies. In the bottom register the king is shown as a bull, presumably destroying the walled town of his enemy. On the other side of the palette Narmer wears the White Crown of Upper Egypt and is clubbing his enemy with a mace

relatively sophisticated activities and achievements of the next five hundred years covered by the four following dynasties of the Old Kingdom. The evidence for this is exemplified by the imposing complex of buildings surrounding the Step Pyramid at Saqqara (plate 10), the forerunner of the great pyramids at Giza. It was built for King Djoser of the Third Dynasty by his architect, Imhotep, whose genius was such that his fame lasted through subsequent ages until he was worshipped as a god, and pilgrimages were still being made to his tomb to seek his reputed powers of healing more than 2,000 years later when he was identified by the Greeks with their own god of healing, Asklepios.

The Step Pyramid which Imhotep designed to be the last resting place of his master, King Djoser, is probably the oldest stone monument in the world to be built on such a scale, and with its maze of underground chambers and passages, its surrounding chapels and shrines, enclosed by a wall which reached 33 feet in height and had a peripheral length of some 5,250 feet, it is surely one of the most remarkable and arresting structures of antiquity. Originally finished in gleaming white limestone, the base of the pyramid itself measured about 358 feet from north to south, and about 410 feet from east to west. The enclosure wall, recessed and panelled to imitate the façade of the king's palace, resembles the walls of the First and Second Dynasty mastabas and this "palace façade" pattern recurs again and again in buildings and shrines, on coffins and sarcophagi, with the obvious intention of creating an eternal palace for the king. This structure is the culmination in stone of the primitive mud-brick and reed buildings of predynastic times and could only have become possible through the existence of an established culture, which included stone working, sculpture, and hieroglyphic writing of a high order.

The Step Pyramid itself, in which Djoser was undoubtedly buried, is the first known of its kind and developed from the earlier type of mastaba tomb built like a platform with sloping sides. It gives the impression of five mastabas one on top of the other, each diminishing in size and resembling a gigantic staircase leading up to the sky, which may have been the intention. From the step pyramid form of the Third Dynasty emerged the true pyramid, which was evolved at the beginning of the Fourth Dynasty to become perfected in the three famous pyramids of Giza.

The buildings surrounding the Step Pyramid represent chapels and shrines for the gods of the various nomes or provinces of Egypt, no doubt symbolizing those in which the king had actually performed the necessary propitiatory ceremonies during his

Limestone sarcophagus carved to represent the façade of the royal palace. Old Kingdom

Left. King Djoser of the Third Dynasty. *Right.* Red granite statue of Bedjmes, a ship-builder of the Third Dynasty

lifetime for the stabilization and good of the country. The building on the east side of the pyramid leads into a long shaft which in turn descends to the interior of the structure and to the burial chambers of the king and the members of his family, and is the prototype of the temples attached to later pyramid tombs. Beside it is the serdab, or statue-chamber, containing the portrait-statue of the king with a slit at eye-level through which he could gaze forth at the offerings made to him by the priests attached to his tomb. This statue is a striking example of the strong and vigorous sculpture of this early period of which all too little survives, and its almost brutal force conveys at the same time a striking impression of majesty: there is no doubt of the divinity of Djoser, or that he was different from ordinary mortals. Whatever scepticism may have assailed later generations regarding the divinity of kingship with the inevitable development of progressive thought and experience of the king's human frailties, the belief at that time in the king as an incarnate god who controlled the destiny of his people was absolute.

The whole purpose of this extraordinarily elaborate project was to maintain a gigantic and effective symbol of the kingship and its function, and to ensure that the rituals and ceremonies necessary for the good of the people should continue for eternity.

Impressive as are the remains of Djoser's pyramid complex even now, largely owing to the remarkable reconstruction work which has been taking place over the past thirty to forty years, the effect in its pristine state, must have been truly awe-inspiring.

An interesting feature about the Saqqara buildings is the reproduction in stone of materials previously used for building, such as the bundles of reeds or papyrus stalks used as supports for walls (plate 6), and wooden logs for lintels and rounded wooden beams for roofing. Even the wooden palisades of earlier times are faithfully reproduced on a solid stone wall, although their original function was no longer required. Wall hangings of mats made from woven reeds or papyrus are reproduced in some of the underground chambers by small glazed tiles of a brilliant blue. The whole structure provides a study of forms which the new materials inspired. Although many of the intervening stages of the development from these early experiments in stone architecture are lost to us, the results are abundantly clear in the later monuments of the New Kingdom and Late Period, and many of the features found for the first time in the buildings of Djoser were destined to become enriched and perfected in the type of architecture which Egypt made so much her own.

It can be inferred from the somewhat scanty evidence available that the Third Dynasty kings chose officials for their intrinsic merit to administer what was a predominantly agricultural economy with well-organized workshops for the production of stone and metal objects and for shipbuilding. Such a one was Bedjmes, the shipbuilder. The construction of such buildings as the Step Pyramid also argues an efficient technical and administrative control of labour, and of mining and quarrying, some of which was carried out at far distances from the capital, and even beyond the frontiers of Egypt in the Sinai Peninsula and in Nubia.

In the Fourth and succeeding Dynasties of the Old Kingdom the administration of the country was held firmly and exclusively in the hands of members of the king's immediate family, into which it was necessary to marry in order to acquire high office in the State. It is at this period that the time-honoured office of the Vizier comes into prominence. A close blood relation of the king, the Vizier was the most important man in the land, second only to the monarch – a veritable Pooh-Bah, judging by the departments of state which were his sole responsibility. Mereruka, for example, whose tomb at Saqqara is one of the best known and shows some of the liveliest scenes of Old Kingdom life, held simultaneously the titles of Vizier, Inspector of Priests of the Pyramid of Teti, Scribe of the Divine Books, Overseer of the King's record-scribes, and Overseer of every work of the King, and there is every reason to believe that they were not all purely honorific – as so often happened in later generations by virtue of ancestral claims to titles long since extinct or of no practical meaning.

In addition there were other important and minor officials who looked after the provisioning, clothing, furnishing and general running of the Palace and the Court. Each king kept a harem of women, so there were plenty of princes available to keep these offices within the royal circle, and it was to their common advantage to preserve the family interests intact. The son of the chief queen was the legitimate heir to the throne, and this queen was doubtless chosen as much for her blood connections as for her charms; nevertheless there must have been many rivalries among the various princes and princesses, and there are signs that conspiracies within the harem may account for sudden changes in the succession or even in the dynasty.

It can only have been this rigid centralization of power that made possible constructional work on a scale of the three great pyramids of Giza. The greatest of them was built for Cheops, or, to give him his Egyptian name, Khufu, and called for the resources of every department of the country, both material and human. This gigantic achievement, together with the erection of the other two slightly smaller pyramids built by his successors Khafrē (Chephren) and Menkaurē (Mycerinus) at Giza, stand for all time as proof of a stable and sublime autocracy, unique in Egyptian history and made possible by social and economic conditions that were never to be repeated.

It is no longer generally accepted that such works were accomplished by slave labour under a barbaric and cruel régime. They were more probably the expression of an implicit belief in the efficacy of maintaining the divine rôle of an all-dispensing, if demanding, Providence in the person of the king. Enormous gangs of labourers, craftsmen, architects, supervisors and sculptors were required to build the Pyramids which, according to Greek writers, took twenty years or so in the making, mostly without any mechanical tackle apart from copper chisels and other simple tools, wooden sledges for conveying the blocks of stone across the desert, and wooden levers for heaving them into place. Plumb-rules and set-squares were used, examples having been found in the vicinity of other pyramids. The exact method of construction has never been entirely satisfactorily explained, although research during recent years has provided the nearest answer to this age-old puzzle that will probably ever be found.

The granite blocks, weighing between $2\frac{1}{2}$ and 15 tons, were dressed by hand with stone pounders, hundreds of which have been found in the vicinity of the desert plateau at Giza. The total area of Khufu's pyramid, the largest of the three, covers more than thirteen acres and the pyramid originally rose to a height of about 481 feet. The original fine white limestone casing has practically disappeared, leaving the inner casing of stone blocks exposed, and these have acquired a soft honey-coloured hue from the sand which has blown against them through the ages.

The pyramid of Khufu at Giza

The vast labour forces required were readily available during the inundation season, when work on the land was suspended and the peasants would otherwise have been idle. The workmen were paid in rations of food and clothing, and no doubt every hand was mobilized in the immense undertaking. This is borne out by names of a nautical character given to some of the working shifts, such as the "starboard" and "larboard" watches, and the "bow" and "stern" watches, implying that some of the Nile sailors were involved. The men were organized into working parties of two hundred or more divided into four shifts to ensure uninterrupted output; the names under which the gangs were identified have been found written in red ochre or incised on the stone blocks. One such gang is called "The crew, Khufu excites love", and others are "The crew, Menkaurē is drunk", "The crew, the White Crown of Khufu is powerful". This gives the impression, in theory at least, of a fairly cooperative attitude inherent in the effort expended on this national enterprise. Small subdivisions of the gangs were named "Antelope gang", "Ibis gang", and so on, which may indicate the regions whence they were levied since the country was divided into nomes or provinces named after the local deity connected with the worship of some animal standard belonging to primitive cults of prehistoric times.

The buildings attached to the Giza Pyramids typify the layout of royal tombs following that of Djoser. A lower temple at the edge of the cultivation and the desert was approached by water and here rites connected with the embalming of the king probably took place. From this temple a covered causeway, whose walls were decorated with reliefs, ran westwards up to a second temple before the pyramid itself. This temple was connected to the pyramid by a false door through which the king was supposed to come forth to partake of the offerings and ceremonies performed in the temple. Nearby were one or more subsidiary pyramids in which were buried the queens or close members of the royal family. On one side of Khufu's pyramid were built the mastaba tombs of the royal princes and princesses and other relatives, while on the other extended the streets of mastabas of the courtiers anxious to continue enjoying the efficacious protection and proximity of their divine master. From the inscriptions and reliefs in these tombs much has been gathered of the biographies of some of these Old Kingdom courtiers, and of their living conditions.

Beside the lower valley temple of Khafrē, the only one of which any substantial remains survive, was carved the Sphinx out of a natural outcrop of rock whose shape suggested the lion's body, which was given a human face, presumed to be that of Khafrē.

The spirit of the Old Kingdom is exemplified in the monuments, inscriptions and sculpture of this period. The calm certainty and composure, the clear uncomplicated lines, convey an optimism and complacency that bear witness to an implicit confidence in the *status quo*. Moreover, the well-fed, prosperous-looking individuals point to a thriving society unimpeded by wars or strife any more serious than the necessity of guarding the frontiers against nomadic tribesmen, or of minor punitive forays across the borders to protect the expeditions which journeyed to Sinai to obtain turquoise, and south into Nubia for other commodities to enrich life, and for building the monuments of the king.

The capital was still at Memphis, the more distant parts of the country being ruled on the king's behalf by trusted and loyal servants, who were maintained and endowed with land by the king's bounty according to their status. By the end of the Old Kingdom, however, these provincial princes or nomarchs became increasingly independent of the royal authority and claimed more prerogatives, waxing rich and powerful on their estates where they ruled like minor kinglets and which accumulated to be handed on from father to son. This state of affairs progressed until, after the death of Pepi II of the Sixth Dynasty (*c.* 2181 B.C.), who reigned for some ninety years and enjoyed what must be the longest reign in history, the central power was finally overthrown, bringing to an end what was considered by later generations to be a golden age to be looked back upon with nostalgia in later more troubled times.

The Old Kingdom is known largely through the preservation of its memory and achievements by later generations, and was the norm to which they always returned as the criterion of what the right order should be. Needless to say, its essence was never recaptured, nor the spontaneous vivacity and sincerity which animated its sculptured

Plate 7. Relief work of the Nineteenth Dynasty, from the temple of Sety I at Abydos, showing the goddess Isis wearing the vulture head-dress surmounted by the moon between cow's horns, the emblems of Hathor, a goddess with whom Isis was associated. She holds a sistrum with the face of Hathor with ears of a cow

reliefs and monuments, though its influence coloured every aspect of life until the end of Egyptian history.

The literature of the Old Kingdom is chiefly known through its preservation in later periods, and it embodied the didactic maxims of wise men concerning the best way to get on in life, precepts of etiquette and good behaviour, and legendary tales about its kings and princes which became classics to be taught in the schools for their content and style for ever afterwards. The only contemporary survivals from this period, apart from some fragmentary texts on papyrus, are the Pyramid Texts, hieroglyphic inscriptions first found carved on the walls of the pyramid of Unas, a king of the Fifth Dynasty, and subsequently forming part of the essential funeral liturgy in royal pyramids and tombs. These texts were eventually adapted for the use of ordinary people, and were written on coffins and on rolls of papyrus which were placed with the dead man or woman in the tomb. They embody the myths and beliefs relating to the king's destiny after death, according to the theory of the sun-religion developed by the priests of the great centre of sun-worship at Heliopolis, and they describe how the dead king might ascend to the sky to join the sun-god Rē, to sail with him in his solar boat through the heavens by day, and through the dark regions of the Underworld by night, rising with him anew each morning. The meanings of these Pyramid Texts are not only baffling to us, they were obscure to the Egyptians themselves, especially after a long period of time, although they were preserved and perpetuated by virtue of their age-old sanctity and magical efficacy.

Grain is almost synonymous with Egypt, and the majority of the population were farmers, whether as freeholders of a small plot of land, or as a kind of serf to the large estate-owners or the estates attached to the Crown or the temples. Ploughing was done with a wooden plough drawn by oxen, and when the grain was ripe it was cut with short scythes just below the heads, laid in bundles on the ground and gathered by women into baskets which were then carried on poles to the threshing floor by men. The workers often paused to rest, or to refresh themselves with water or beer while women and children followed the harvesters gleaning. The grain was trodden out by oxen or sheep, and after being separated, it was winnowed with flat scoops by being thrown high into the air so that the dust was blown away by the wind.

The land in theory was the gift of the king as personifying the god Horus, and the large temples built and endowed by him were run by a priesthood which deputized for the monarch in performing the essential daily and seasonal rites and ceremonies before the gods which were necessary for the wellbeing of the community. Apart from the professional priests, it appears that the royal family and the nobility held priestly offices and performed duties in the temples on behalf of the king at stated times and at regular intervals, combining them with other offices and functions.

The professional priesthood comprised the intellectual element of the community, and were responsible for conserving and accumulating knowledge, preserving the traditions and literature of past ages, and for furthering and fostering progress in all branches of science and learning. The temple was not only the house of the god, but also the repository of historical archives, state records, and rolls of the law; and in the "House of Life" attached to it were educated the sons of the aristocracy, the scribes, and future government officials. The estates and farms attached to the temples rendered

Plate 8. The mummified god Osiris, holding the crook and flail, emblems of fertility and hence symbols of kingship

The middle aisle of the pillared hall of the Lower Temple of Khafrē, at Giza. The well-proportioned columns are of unadorned red granite

The Sphinx and Pyramid of Khufu at Giza

Above top. Section of the Pyramid Texts, from the Pyramid of Unas at Saqqara. *Above.* Painted harvest scene from the Eighteenth-Dynasty tomb of Menna, who watches the work from a kiosk (top left)

them self-supporting for supplies of necessary food offerings, animal sacrifices, and other equipment for the maintenance of the gods' cult and for the resident priests and minor officials and servants connected with them. Workshops were also attached to the temples from which came the best work of the sculptors, metalworkers, goldsmiths and carpenters, for the furnishings and adornment of the temple, the royal palace and the royal tombs.

The king owned the land of Egypt by virtue of his personification with the god Horus, the son of Osiris. According to tradition, Horus and his brother, Seth, were originally awarded the two parts of Egypt after a tribunal of gods had pronounced judgment on their dispute over its possession. It is perhaps possible to see in this legend the rival contentions of prehistoric followers of two tribal cults representing the northern and southern parts of the country prior to its unification under one king. Seth took the form of a strange composite animal, probably incorporating the characteristics of several tribal gods, while Horus originated as a falcon god, hence the falcon was one of the pictorial representations of royalty. The character of Horus was unimpeachable, while Seth seems to have had a dual personality and represented the darker side of life – he was the god of the desert – but at times he assumed a more respectable character and was venerated by certain dynasties of kings who originated from those parts of the country where Seth was worshipped, and who incorporated his name into their own, notably the rulers of the Nineteenth Dynasty named Sethos, or Sety.

It was the king's responsibility as the living Horus, and as the physical agent through which life flowed from the gods, to build and maintain the temples and to endow them with estates in proportion to their size and importance in order to maintain the cult of the gods who demanded the same material sustenance and equipment as physical beings, and in order to ensure the equilibrium of the world for the sake of the community at large. The notion of thousands of men toiling in blind servility for a despotic tyrant, which the contemplation of the gigantic monuments dedicated to the might of pharaoh formerly evoked, seems incompatible with what is now known from later interpretations of the records about the true motives behind these works. In devoting their lives, work, skill and genius to the glorification of the pharaoh, the Egyptians were in fact only working for their own preservation and wellbeing, either consciously, or merely because it was the way of their world.

In addition to the temple endowments, the gifts of land made to their regional representatives by successive kings, whether from bounty or expediency, ultimately led to a situation which upset the balance of power, and enabled the increasingly powerful landowners to wield undue influence over the throne, giving rise to the anomaly that the real owner and dispenser of land became dependent on his beneficiaries to maintain his own position. The logical result was revolution.

Chapter Four

THE MIDDLE KINGDOM

"I am meditating upon what has happened, on the things that have come to pass throughout the land. Changes take place; it is not like last year, and one year is more burdensome than the other. The land is in confusion. . . . Right is cast out and iniquity is in the council chamber. The plans of the gods are destroyed, and their ordinances transgressed. The land is in misery, mourning is in every place, towns and villages lament. . . ."

Thus a pessimistic writer described the state into which Egypt had fallen during the 150 years or so between the collapse of the Old Kingdom and the rise of the Middle Kingdom. During this unsettled time the local princes ruled independently, warring with one another and eventually forming alliances which resolved themselves into two main confederacies, one ruling from Heracleopolis, just south of the Faiyûm, the other, which was eventually to triumph, from Thebes. It was a powerful princely family from Thebes, named Mentuhotpe, who finally led the southerners to victory and who formed the Eleventh Dynasty. These self-styled kings of Upper and Lower Egypt justified this title in fact when about 2050 B.C. Mentuhotpe II gained control of the whole country, took the name of "He-who-unites-the-Two-Lands", and launched the beginning of the Middle Kingdom period.

In spite of these upheavals, Thebes and other districts where the local nomarchs remained stable and wealthy enough, maintained the old way of life. As Thebes waxed powerful, and artists and sculptors continued to be employed on monumental works for the ruling classes, new elements appeared, particularly in mural painting of tomb scenes which had previously been carved in relief, and a freer expression of detail became apparent. The social upheaval created an opportunity for the emergence of those sections of the population which had previously been subjected to unquestioning obedience and direction from above into a middle class of artisans, craftsmen and tradesmen of all kinds between the feudal aristocracy and the peasant population, who continued to till the land. Some idea of the social revolution which had taken place can perhaps be imagined from the lamentations of the sage already quoted:

"Behold, the poor of the land have become rich; he that possessed clothes is now in rags. He that wove not for himself now possesseth fine linen. . . . Nay but gold and lapis lazuli, silver and turquoise . . . are hung about the necks of slave girls . . . noble ladies walk through the land and mistresses of houses say 'would that we had something we might eat'." Perhaps there is an indication of a wider distribution of the good things of life in "Behold, the bald head that used no oil now possesseth jars of pleasant myrrh" and "he that had no knowledge of harp-playing now possesseth a harp".

The last king of the Eleventh Dynasty sent his Vizier, Amenemhet, on an expedition into the desert east of Coptos along the age-old caravan route in search of the stone and the gold which is still mined there. Amenemhet brought back a splendid block of stone for the king's sarcophagus and received his royal master's praises and rewards; but it was not long afterwards that this able and shrewd man succeeded in usurping the throne and becoming the first king of the Twelfth Dynasty.

The expeditions which went out on missions of this kind were highly organized, the commissariat alone being a triumph of planning to feed and maintain a large body of mining experts, officials, scribes and workmen for long periods in the desert. Teams of donkeys went with them laden with equipment, food, water and sandals, and the inscriptions left by the members of these expeditions on the rocks and in the quarries have many a tale to tell of hardships, successes, and failures. It was not often that the boast could be made that the whole expedition returned without the loss of a single donkey.

Amenemhet transferred the capital to the border of Lower and Middle Egypt, at Lisht, where the kings of the Twelfth Dynasty built their pyramids. There followed a long period of peace, development and consolidation under a strong and energetic line of kings who, while confirming the previous land-owners in their titles and estates, and promoting their own followers to similar positions, at the same time kept them on a tight rein, thus avoiding the situation which arose at the end of the Old Kingdom. The arts and literature flourished to such an extent that the language of the Middle Kingdom became the classical model for all time. The frontiers with Nubia were firmly established by a series of fortresses built at strategic points between the First and Third Cataracts, and a southern boundary was fixed at the Second Cataract after several military expeditions had been sent "to overcome the vile Kush" (Nubia) and a stela was set up and inscribed "to prevent any Nubian from passing it downstream overland or by boat, or any flocks and herds of Nubians, apart from any Nubian who shall come to trade . . . or upon a mission (i.e. anything) that may be done lawfully with them". A collection of despatches from the garrison of one of these fortresses survives, giving daily reports of the movements of Nubians to the Vizier far away in the north of Egypt, and all ending with what was the accepted formula in official communications of this kind: "All the affairs of the King's domain are safe and sound". That there must have been an efficient postal system is evident from the large amount of correspondence that took place between officials and their superiors on matters of state, as well as between private individuals concerning their personal and family affairs. It was probably maintained by a body of couriers, who, no doubt, took advantage of the regular caravans proceeding up and down the country and the even more constant river traffic, the Nile being the main highway for transport of every kind of goods and people. In the New Kingdom there seems to have been a regular postal service with relays of horse-drawn chariots from one part of the country to another. The only documentary evidence in support of this survives in a love letter in which the lover expresses an ardent wish that the beloved could come as quickly as the royal courier for whom horses wait at various stages. Like the master who impatiently awaits the courier, the lovesick heart leaps with joy at his arrival.

In addition to the promotion of foreign trade, large irrigation works were undertaken by the Middle Kingdom rulers, particularly in the neighbourhood of the

Top right. Wooden model of Meketre and his scribes counting his cattle, from his tomb at Thebes (Dyn. XI). *Right*. Detail of painting of offerings on a Middle Kingdom coffin

Faiyûm, and while almost nothing now remains of the great temples of the Middle Kingdom, there is evidence that large-scale building works were undertaken, to judge by the quality of the sculpture that has survived. The minor and applied arts flourished, and the queens and princesses of the Middle Kingdoms were adorned by jewellery of a standard of delicacy and elegant taste which was never surpassed, showing that the goldsmiths and jewellers of that period were pastmasters of their craft. The painters, too, achieved a high standard in the richly decorated tombs of the nobles where the sporting pursuits of the landed gentry are depicted with delightful freshness and grace and with a wealth of observation of the wild life of the marshlands and desert.

It is at this period that were made those enchanting painted wooden models which have been found of domestic scenes of cooking, baking and brewing, harvesting and weaving, which throw so much light on the activities of daily life. These models were placed in the tombs to fulfil the same purpose as the elaborately carved wall scenes of the Old Kingdom mastabas. With the spread of former royal and princely burial practices to wider sections of the population, and the improved conditions of the middle classes, this was probably a less costly method, both in material and space, of satisfying their aspirations for a "goodly burial in the west" than the former grandiose mastabas with their many-chambered tombs of large proportions. The long lines of hieroglyphic funerary texts which appeared on the walls were replaced by painted inscriptions on the large wooden coffins of the period, some of which were very beautifully executed, later to be replaced by a collection of similar texts called the Book of the Dead, written on papyrus and rolled up and placed in the coffin with the deceased along with a collection of accompanying amulets, statuettes, and figures of gods and other effective symbols of magical potency.

Chapter Five

THE NEW KINGDOM

The collapse of the Middle Kingdom, due to a series of weak kings towards the end of the period, was accompanied by the infiltration into the north-east Delta of Semitic nomadic tribes who took advantage of the gradual weakening of the central government in Egypt to establish a separate kingdom in the northern part of the country, while in the south the general pattern was maintained by the able Egyptian viziers and officials who had emerged as the result of the long period of stability under the early Middle Kingdom kings. These foreign rulers, called by the Egyptians "Hyksos", "rulers of foreign countries", were not the ruthless brigands which later Egyptian historians not unnaturally made them out to be, and it appears that they ruled contemporaneously with varying degrees of tolerance together with the native dynasties, while yet another line of kings reigned in Nubia. The Hyksos adopted Egyptian titles, customs and religious practices with Seth as their chief god but, as generally happened under conditions of this nature, there was a decline in the arts and culture generally while the administrative pattern was to a large extent maintained, though upset from time to time when the rival powers collided or rose against one another. It is thought that this state of affairs lasted for about 200 years during which time the old artistic and literary traditions were preserved in some areas and received a new stimulus in places like Thebes whence arose once again a powerful family of princes who, having assumed the title of Kings of Upper and Lower Egypt, were destined eventually to expel once and for all the hated foreigners from Egyptian soil.

It was no doubt under the stress of this period that the Egyptian army, which had hitherto consisted of a sort of feudal militia, controlled and recruited by the central government as and when the need arose, began to evolve as the highly disciplined professional force with which the foreign conquests of the New Kingdom were later to be achieved and maintained. During the Old and Middle Kingdoms the need for military operations had been largely confined to protecting the frontiers, policing the desert routes to the mines and the oases, and carrying out the vast constructional works and the trading and mining expeditions into Nubia, the eastern deserts, and overseas. For this purpose there was always a small regular force, including a *corps d'élite* to guard the palace and the king, largely composed of Nubians and other foreigners settled in Egypt. The well-drilled squadrons were highly trained for all these purposes, a large part of their duties being to know the methods and techniques connected with mining, quarrying and transportation of building stone and other materials, all of which came under the army, organized by army scribes, and supplemented by levies from the landowners' country estates. Their fighting weapons consisted of spears, battle-axes, maces, and bows and arrows.

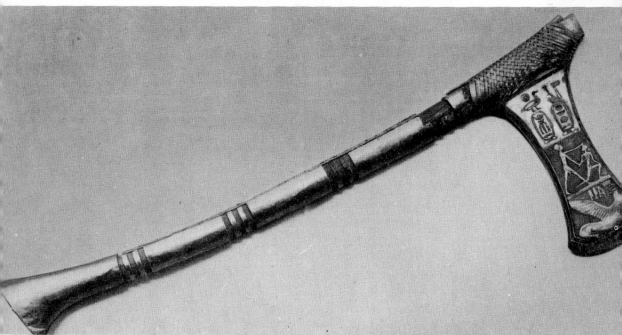

Above top. Bronze head of battle-axe from Semna, Eighteenth Dynasty. *Above.* The ceremonial battle-axe of Amosis I

With the founding of the Eighteenth Dynasty, the beginning of the New Kingdom, by Amosis, who finally expelled the Hyksos in about 1567 B.C., the most spectacular era of Egyptian history began, and with it the rise of a military caste and a permanent army of professional soldiers.

Amosis pursued the Hyksos to their stronghold in southern Palestine, which he took after a siege lasting for three years, thus opening the way for the aggressive policies of the New Kingdom warrior kings and cultivating a taste for foreign conquest so successfully followed up by Tuthmosis I and his successors. The next hundred and thirty years were to witness the growth of an empire which at its furthest extent stretched in the north across the Euphrates and in the south to the Fourth Cataract and beyond.

The army of this period was under the titular command of the king and delegated in practice to a Great General. Infantry companies of two hundred highly efficient men under their own standards drilled and paraded to the sound of the trumpet, and regiments were named after the state gods, Amūn, Rē, Ptah, and Seth. The cream of the army was the chariotry, the horse and chariot being introduced from Asia via Palestine just before the dawn of the New Kingdom and used to great effect in battle. The chariot was a light two-wheeled vehicle made of wood and leather, and drawn by two horses. The warrior and his charioteer rode in it standing up with the reins tied round the body to leave the arms free for fighting and shooting arrows from a composite bow. The kings, many of whom in fact led their armies personally, are depicted charging the enemy at the head of the chariotry and the hail of arrows they discharged was followed up by the infantry in hand-to-hand fighting with spears, swords, and copper and bronze-headed axes. There was no cavalry as such, the only horsemen being scouts and despatch riders.

The Egyptians became famous horse-breeders and the kings maintained magnificent studs, their horses being greatly prized and loved. One warrior pharaoh, on entering a conquered city in Ethiopia, whose subject prince had rebelled against him, was more incensed at finding the horses in his royal stables neglected than at the defiance and treason of the rebel, and he fulminated: "As truly as I live, and as Rē loves me, and my nostrils are rejuvenated with divine life, the fact that *my* horses have been starved is harder for me to bear than all your wicked deeds".

Large numbers of foreign mercenaries were still used in the army, together with Egyptians, the latter distinguished by the Plume of War, an ostrich feather stuck in the hair, this being an age-old ritual custom signifying that a soldier was in action. Another old custom demanded that a formal declaration of war be made before attacking an enemy, and this was adhered to honourably, at least between contending Egyptians, if more wily tactics were resorted to in the case of subduing foreign strongholds. Foreign mercenaries wore helmets or their own national headdress and used their own brand of weapons, and these distinctions are faithfully reproduced in the battle scenes carved on temple walls, as are also the facial characteristics of the different races amongst which can be detected Nubians, Libyans and peoples from the Aegean.

The warriors carried wood and leather shields; and armour in the form of tunics and aprons of leather covered with metal scales was worn.

The scribes, ever ready to denigrate any other profession in order to glorify their own, give terrifying accounts of the hardships of a soldier's life, which are probably not

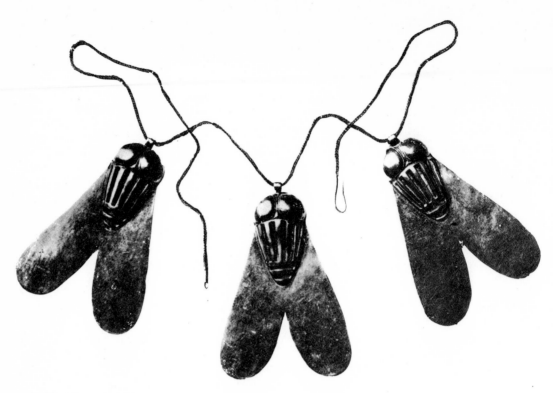

Golden flies awarded as military decorations

entirely unfounded, and they miss no chance of enlarging on the hazards and dangers of war, and of the long desert campaigns when the soldier must "carry his food and drink on his back like a donkey and stops marching only to be on guard", returning home like "worm-eaten wood. He becomes ill and is brought back on a donkey." Be that as it may, the soldier was well rewarded for his valour with plots of tax-free land, slaves, and "the gold of valour" – a military decoration in the form of a golden fly or a golden collar. In peace-time he could relax at home with his family enjoying the best of food and drink, or hold lucrative appointments with the rank of Great Commander, or Royal Scribe. Those with linguistic ability held posts in the colonial service as interpreters, ambassadors or administrators on peace-time diplomatic and trade missions, such posts also including priestly appointments in the temples. The military caste gained great influence as time went on, so much so that positions of great eminence, even the throne itself, could be gained by way of the army.

Oriental diplomacy at this period was a protracted business, hemmed in by symbols and protocol. A great deal was done by sending diplomatic missions to neighbouring powers in Syria and Palestine with threats, cajolery and compliments, supported by bribes and subsidies: and pacts were cemented by diplomatic marriages contracted by the pharaoh with foreign princesses, though Egyptian princesses were never sent abroad for this purpose. The queens also kept up correspondence with one another in support of their husbands' policies and helped to maintain friendly relations between the royal courts. Treaties were drawn up in accordance with a code of international law, which was then universally accepted throughout the Near East, alliances on reciprocal terms, and pacts of "peace and brotherhood" entered into, each party swearing by its own gods to observe them. Official correspondence was carried out in the cuneiform script in Akkadian, the *lingua franca* of the period, and formal modes of address between heads of state strictly adhered to: "My Brother", or "My Servant", according to who was writing; and polite conventional phrases of enquiry after His Majesty's health and wellbeing were essential before getting down to business.

One of the dominant powers at that time was the kingdom of Mitanni in Syria, to the north-west of the Euphrates, which was ruled by dynasties of Aryan stock, later to be succeeded by the Hittites from the north, and the Assyrians. During the New Kingdom Mitanni was in close alliance with Egypt, maintaining trade relations, the Mitannian rulers being eager to acquire Egypt's gold in exchange for their copper; and the alliance was further strengthened by the giving of one of the Mitannian princesses in marriage to the Pharaoh Amenhotpe III. The discovery in 1887 of the diplomatic correspondence between the two courts threw a flood of light on the political situation and the relations between Egypt and her vassals at that period. The letters were written in cuneiform on clay tablets which were accidentally discovered by a peasant woman at the modern village of Amarna in Middle Egypt while collecting dried dung for fuel (following the custom of her ancient ancestors who used it for the same purpose, wood and charcoal being scarce and rationed from government stores). The tablets were thought to be of no value, some being thrown away as rubbish and others sold for a song, but their importance was eventually realized by scholars and they were translated.

The Eighteenth Dynasty kings following Amosis, the Dynasty's founder, were called Amenhotpe and Tuthmosis, and it was the first Tuthmosis who, in order to prevent further foreign invasions, followed up the incursions into Palestine and Syria made by Amosis after the expulsion of the Hyksos. He carried out a successful expedition to the Euphrates, which he crossed, and the kingdoms and principalities of that region acknowledged Egypt's supremacy, paying tribute to the Pharaoh who left Egyptian representatives to control the conquered territories under their own native rulers. At the same time the first reigns of the dynasty were marked by restoring and consolidating a once more united kingdom at home, the main consequences being renewed activity in repairing old temples and building new ones, thus forging the chain of the established order of stability between the gods and mankind, a major item of political expediency. Foremost among these were the temples at Karnak and Luxor, the former having been founded in the Middle Kingdom and added to by succeeding generations of Egyptian kings up to the Roman period. Karnak became the centre *par excellence* of the state cult of Amon-rē, remaining as a veritable historical document in stone for posterity.

The son of Tuthmosis I, who had been married to his sister Hatshepsut probably for dynastic reasons, a not uncommon practice among Egyptian royalty, reigned for only eight years, and was succeeded by the young son of a concubine also called Tuthmosis. It appears that Hatshepsut, the widowed queen, who bore to the young king the relationship of aunt and step-mother by virtue of her marriage to her brother and his father, considered she had an equal right to the throne and was supported by a large faction of the powerful priesthood of Amon-rē. At first she ruled as regent for the

Left. Queen Hatshepsut in male dress. *Right*. Black granite statuette of Senenmut, with the princess on his lap

68

young Tuthmosis, and later succeeded in securing her coronation as full king of Upper and Lower Egypt, keeping Tuthmosis in obscurity for many years. It is probable that the equal strength of his claim to the throne induced her to emphasize her kingship by assuming male titles, using the masculine pronoun in her inscriptions, and wearing male costume, at least on her statues and monuments. The family feud was at length resolved either by her deposition or by her death some twenty years later when Tuthmosis III came at last into his heritage and became one of the most spectacular of Egypt's warrior kings.

During Hatshepsut's reign there was no war-mongering and Egypt enjoyed a period of peace and prosperity when the arts and trade flourished and grand architectural projects were fostered. The Queen's favourite minister, Senenmut, wielded great power and was at the head of most of her great undertakings, notably as the architect of her magnificent temple at Deir el-Bahri, on the west bank of the Nile at Thebes, on the walls of which are carved with the highest technical mastery detailed scenes of out-standing events of her reign, including an expedition organized by the ubiquitous Senenmut to Punt, where trade with the natives of this land, believed to be somewhere on the Somali coast, secured a cargo of incense trees, wood, animal skins and other luxuries for the adornment of Hatshepsut's court.

Also depicted on her temple walls is the transport of a pair of granite obelisks from Aswan, which were to be set up in the temple of Karnak to celebrate her jubilee in the sixteenth year of her reign; one of them still stands inscribed with the queen's name and titles. The obelisk stands 97 feet high and weighs about 320 tons, and this single block of granite was quarried in one piece with its fellow, and was transported down the Nile from Aswan to Thebes, dressed, inscribed and erected in seven months from start to finish. Such is the tenor of the inscription carved on its base, and the account of this great achievement ends in Hatshepsut's words: "Let not him who hears this say that what I have said is a lie, but rather let him say 'How like her it is!'."

Obelisks are a distinctive architectural feature of Egypt, derived from an ancient cult symbol at Heliopolis, the home of the sun-religion. The form spread all over Egypt in the Old Kingdom, and obelisks were often placed in pairs at the entrances to tombs and temples. They varied in size from the modest pair found on either side of the door-ways of private tombs to the enormous examples erected before the great temples by different monarchs. These consisted of a tapering block of granite surmounted by a pyramidal apex cased in electrum, a natural alloy of silver and gold, that gleamed in the rays of the sun. The monolithic blocks were levered out of the Aswan quarries with large tree trunks, hoisted on to sledges and dragged to the river bank where they were manhandled on to barges and borne down the Nile to their destination. The majority of the largest surviving obelisks are now far from their native land, adorning European capitals, in Rome, Paris and London. The famous "Cleopatra's Needle", which stands on the Thames Embankment in London, is, in fact, inscribed with the name of Tuthmosis III.

Hatshepsut's temple itself is an architectural masterpiece, designed with an inspired regard for its setting in a natural bay of the towering cliffs of the western desert at Thebes, and even in its present ruined state is one of the most impressive sights in Egypt. The architect and organizer of all this activity, Senenmut, also acted as tutor to the royal princess, and is seen dandling the little girl on his knee, no doubt inculcating her with suitable maxims from the traditional books of wisdom written by the Egyptian sages. Such was his importance at court that he even inserted portraits of himself in discreet corners of the Queen's temple, an unheard-of privilege – or audacity – and had two tombs built for himself, one, which was never finished, in the actual precincts of the temple. He was an example of how a man of humble origin could, through ability and hard work, coupled no doubt with a fair share of opportunism and of personal influence, attain to the highest position by way of the army in which he had served as a royal scribe, ultimately gaining the confidence and favour of the Queen. He disappears with her, and it is likely that his downfall occurred when Tuthmosis III came to power, in view of his second unfinished tomb, and the obliteration in the first of his name and titles. It can be imagined how the Queen and all her followers were abhorred by Tuthmosis, and became the subjects of his vindictiveness, which is amply borne out by the systematic erasure of Hatshepsut's name wherever it appeared, and the usurpation of her monuments by himself or with the name of his father.

As soon as he came to the throne Tuthmosis immediately took to the field to re-establish Egypt's supremacy in Palestine where the vassal states were showing signs of rebellion. Following up his successes by a brilliant series of campaigns, he extended his authority north of the Euphrates as far as the boundaries of the increasingly powerful Hittite kingdom. His military exploits are described in scenes and inscriptions in temples and on stelae throughout Egypt and leave an impression of a military genius and an outstanding personality. His statues show a man of determination and character, not without a sense of humour.

These were the days of Egypt's splendour and unquestioned superiority in the ancient world, and the tombs of the great viziers and generals and other officials of the period demonstrate the tributes in material wealth and in prestige which flowed into Egypt from all sides. The upper classes enjoyed affluent and luxurious living, while the middle classes, artisans, government and temple scribes, and the farmers, must all have shared in the general prosperity and the assured position which a dominant nation enjoys.

For a brief period between 1379 and 1362 B.C. there emerges a personality in the shape of the then reigning king, Akhenaten, that is unique in Egyptian history. Akhenaten was, according to whichever way he is regarded, a visionary intellectual, born ages before his time, or a physically deformed religious crank. Whatever view is held, he was an iconoclast, and evolved a religious doctrine of the worship of the sun's disc, the Aten, identified with himself, as the sole source of life to the exclusion not only of the supreme state god, Amon-rē, but of all the other gods. In spite of the apparent monotheism of this idea, there are indications that much of his doctrine was based on the age-old sun-religion of Heliopolis. That Akhenaten was a cultivated scholar is evident from the hymns to the Aten which are attributed to him, but he finally carried his fanaticism to the extent of breaking away from the traditional beliefs practised by the priesthood of Amūn at Thebes and transferring his capital to a hitherto virgin site where the modern village of Amarna now stands. Here he built an entirely new city for himself and Nefertiti, his beautiful queen, and his followers, and erected temples to his chosen deity, fully open to the sky to receive the direct benefit of the sun's

Plate 9. Painted limestone statue of Queen Tetisheri, maternal grandmother of Amosis, the founder of the Eighteenth Dynasty. She is depicted as a young woman with the vulture head-dress worn by queens

rays, as distinct from the dark and secret sanctuaries of Amūn. His esoteric doctrine was never accepted by, if it was ever intended for, the mass of the people and, of course, it was abhorred by the traditionalists. The concentration on the life-giving aspect of the sun's disc and the religious conception of the Aten through which all forms of life and nature were quickened coincided with a period when the Egyptians had reached what was probably the highest and most sophisticated peak of their cultural development, and the effect on the art and literature of the period, which had for a long time been developing freer and more naturalistic tendencies, was dramatic. While the old traditions continued to evolve more naturally, the Court art of Amarna, in deference to the Pharaoh's ideas and inspiration, shows an individuality and originality which in its early stages is a refreshing innovation on the stereotyped Egyptian formalism, but which was pushed to such exaggerated limits that it became grotesque. Yet its influence continued to be felt long after Akhenaten's memory had been ruthlessly and deliberately obliterated as though he had never existed.

His end is unknown, and the Court returned to Thebes during the reign of his successor Tutankhamūn, a boy king who soon fell once more under the sway of the traditional régime and whose name was to become a household word in the twentieth century A.D. through the discovery of his intact tomb by the English archaeologist, Howard Carter. The priests of Amūn, having restored the right order to Egypt, swept away all trace of the hated heretic and levelled his city to the ground. Owing to the anathema of the spot, nothing was ever built over the site and its foundations therefore remain the only complete example from which it has been possible to reconstruct an Egyptian city of the New Kingdom.

Owing to Akhenaten's preoccupation with religion and philosophical theorizing to the exclusion of all else, Egypt's foreign dependencies in Syria and Palestine had got out of control, and had only been kept together by the ability and energy of Akhenaten's Great General in Lower Egypt, Horemheb. After acting as one of the chief advisers to Tutankhamūn, Horemheb gained the throne for himself and by his reforms and firm administration restored the country to its former prosperity and stability, which he ensured by promoting the candidature of a military family from the Delta called Ramesses to succeed him, thus founding the line of kings of that name whose colossal monuments have earned for them perpetual and popular fame as the greatest pharaohs of Egypt. In fact, the Ramessid period held the seeds of the decline of the truly great days of Egypt, which are spanned by the kings of the previous dynasty, from about 1567 B.C. until Ramesses III of the Twentieth Dynasty (1198–1166 B.C.).

The status of Egypt was maintained during the hundred and fifty years after the restoration of the old order following the Akhenaten heresy and during the reigns of the early Ramessids whose colossal monuments survive all over Egypt, among the most notable being the great Hypostyle Hall in Karnak Temple, the Ramesseum and Medinet Habu temples at Thebes, and the temples of Abu Simbel.

The growing threat of invasions from the Hittites and the Aegean Sea Peoples more than once gave rise to land and sea battles on a large scale which, combined with a series of weak kings towards the end of the Ramessid period who in fact ruled through the powerful priesthood of Amūn, started the decline from world power from which Egypt never fully recovered.

Plate 10. King Djoser's Step Pyramid at Saqqara. On the right can be seen one of the papyrus columns reproduced in stone

Left. Luxor Temple: obelisk of Ramesses II before the principal pylon, which shows traces of the cavetto cornice. *Right.* Queen Hatshepsut's temple at Deir el-Bahari, Thebes

Top right. King Tuthmosis III (*left*); and King Akhenaten, from a pillar statue at Karnak. *Right.* Unfinished head of Queen Nefertiti from a sculptor's workshop at Amarna

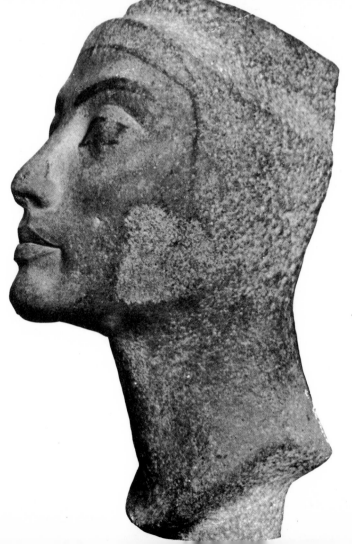

Left. An ivory label showing King Den of the First Dynasty. The hieroglyphs read: "The first time of smiting the East", which probably refers to an expedition to Sinai. *Right.* Ramesses II smiting Nubian prisoners, whom he holds by the hair. He wears the Double Crown of Upper and Lower Egypt, and carries a bow and arrows. From the Temple of Abu Simbel

The Egyptian attitude to war was not that of an aggressive people loving war for its own sake. Theoretically they believed that Egypt represented the cosmic order as laid down by the gods at the time of creation, and insofar as other countries departed from or resisted this norm, or failed to subscribe to pharaoh's organized rule, they represented the forces of chaos which must be brought into line under his beneficent domination; hence the conventional representation of the king trampling his enemies underfoot, and the rows of bound foreign captives symbolizing conquered foreign lands being brought into the enclosing circle of the Egyptian order. The king embodied Egypt's triumph in war as in everything else; he was the "Commander-in-chief of his army, valiant in his chariot, who seizes his bow and shoots straight, never missing his target; the one who holds his ground, magnificent in his bravery; his strong arm carries the mace and the shield, he tramples kings under his foot and knows no retreat". He was depicted larger than anyone else in the battle scenes, supported in the rear by his armies a fraction of his size, leading his troops into the fray and subduing the enemy single-handed by his divine might. That this ideal was lived up to to a large extent, we know from the exploits recorded of the various warrior kings on the temple walls and on stelae. Ramesses II and Ramesses III were particularly addicted to recording their triumphs in all the main temples of Egypt, particularly at Medinet Habu and at Karnak. In practice the time came when they had to defend the frontiers against invasions from the increasing power of neighbouring eastern states, who coveted Egypt's wealth and prosperous fertility, such as the Hittites in the New Kingdom, and later the Assyrians and Persians who actually succeeded in conquering Egypt during the period of her decline. For many generations, however, Egypt's might and well-organized armies succeeded in maintaining her sway and defending her foreign colonies.

An epic poem left by Ramesses II concerning a battle he fought at Kadesh in Syria, where he extricated himself and his army by his personal courage and resource from a tight corner, has survived in a papyrus which is supplemented by the explanatory which are given in great detail in many temples including that at Luxor and the which are given in great detail in many temples including those at Luxor and the Ramesseum at Thebes.

Kadesh, a small principality under Egyptian suzerainty, was situated at a strategic position on the river Orontes and had fallen to the Hittites, then becoming a great power in north-western Syria, and Ramesses set out to recapture it. He took with him the regiments of Amūn, Ptah, Rē and Seth, and spies from the enemy camp appeared offering to join Ramesses' army, saying they had deserted, and giving false information as to the enemy's position. Acting on this, Ramesses pressed on towards the town and crossed the river with only a few personal followers, outstripping the army of Amūn which was following behind him. While the main army were busy pitching their camp, Ramesses sat on his throne at rest, the division of Rē crossing the river, and the other two divisions straggling in the rear, that of Seth still marching far back on the road approaching it. The Hittite army was in fact drawn up just behind the city and officers came running to warn Ramesses, having caught two Hittite scouts whom they interrogated with severe beatings and from whom they extracted the true whereabouts of the enemy. Meanwhile the Hittites had advanced round the city and almost succeeded

Ramesses III, dismounted from his chariot, shoots at enemy ships in a naval battle. Below, Egyptian soldiers lead away their captives

in cutting off Ramesses from his men, who seem to have panicked. Ramesses sent his Vizier to warn the armies of Ptah and Seth to make all haste to his support. Then he called on his father, Amūn, and said that "though alone and deserted by my army, he came to my aid". Hastily donning his armour he charged the enemy alone in his chariot at the gallop, drawn by his great horse Victory-in-Thebes, a thoroughbred from the royal stable. He declares that, single-handed, he captured 2,500 Hittite chariots and flung the enemy into the Orontes, the Hittite chief shrinking in fear and wonder before him. Only his charioteer, his butler, and his faithful horse remained by his side, and he gives vent to bitter reproaches to his armies for forsaking him. Whatever the true facts of the case, and allowing for its enlargement into epic proportions for the sake of the records, he seems to have fought his way out of the impasse with commend-able courage, while allied reinforcements fortunately arrived in time to avert a complete Egyptian disaster. Whether the victory claimed was as complete as he makes out, his personal exploit seems to be true enough.

Chapter Six

SOCIETY

The structure of society in Egypt changed very little during the three thousand years of its history, the general pattern being disturbed only by the two intermediate revolutionary periods, and for not more than a couple of decades during the Amarna interlude which, because of its total aberration from the Egyptian norm, is sometimes given an isolated prominence for this very reason.

The normal shape of Egyptian society was itself rather like a pyramid, with the pharaoh as the apex, represented next by the Vizier for the administration, the High Priest of the current state god for the clergy and maintenance of the cult – so vital a part of the social and economic structure – and the Chief Commander of the Army, for military duties, national security, and organization of building projects and expeditions for raw materials. The king was in actual fact the head of every department, and delegated his duties to these three chief deputies, who were in turn each supported by a host of officials in descending grades forming a vast bureaucracy of scribes, archivists, master masons, skilled artisans, agricultural overseers and the like. The base of the pyramid was the peasant population who laboured in the fields, on the building sites, in the workshops and on the dykes and canals. All were responsible to the king, and all were paid by him in kind and in bounty, with large estates, rich tombs and burial equipment, and gifts of gold and other luxuries for the high officials; and in wages of vegetables, oil and clothing for the workers.

Many class differences and conflicts existed, together with a good deal of snobbery, but there was a sense of common social justice and rights due to rich and poor alike. The different professions and trades tended to marry within their own circles and to keep their class privileges intact; though it was possible for those with exceptional talent and ability to win royal favour and to be elevated to the highest positions in the land. For others, who were not quite so gifted, a way to advancement lay in the time-honoured method, which does not seem to have changed, of bribery and personal influence. To gain a place of favour in the heart of the king was a commonly voiced aspiration equivalent to a healthy desire to progress in life.

On the whole, the State seems to have been a benignant despotism in duty bound to look after the poorer people in times of stress and famine. Many are the records which describe the distribution of corn from the State granaries in the lean years following a series of poor inundations.

The very good life led by the nobility is exemplified in their tomb scenes for all to see; but there is not much to show how the lower strata of society lived, since they were buried in pits in the sand or in communal graves with only their humble personal possessions or trinkets. It should not be taken for granted that the happy workers seen on the tomb walls singing in the fields as they toiled so cheerfully and energetically for their masters present an entirely true picture, for life must have been hard for the peasants; but there is little doubt that the peasant population, and the serfs and slaves, were better fed than their present-day descendants and, in spite of the undoubted hardships of their lot, they probably possessed the same happy temperament which accepted it all with fatalistic cheerfulness and good humour.

Slavery existed insofar as foreign captives, prisoners of war, and some Egyptians could be owned by the State, the temple priesthoods, and private individuals, and could be sold, bequeathed or hired. They had, however, certain legal rights and could own property and land and marry freeborn women, and they could also be emancipated by an official act.

The landed estates employed a labour force of serfs by a kind of feudal system, since the serfs seem to have owned cattle and small plots of land themselves, and were subject to tax on its produce. The tax-gatherers were as dreaded and unpopular as they are now, though the methods of dealing with false returns or recalcitrant payers were somewhat more crude: the unhappy victims were beaten until they paid up.

The State's capital consisted largely of agricultural produce and herds of cattle, and the administration for tax collection, if highly complicated, was also very efficient, employing a vast number of officials, recorders, and scribes of accounts, the Egyptian being a dedicated keeper of written records in every conceivable department of life.

Egypt was self-supporting except for serviceable timber, bronze, silver, lapis lazuli, and certain spices and oils, which were obtained from abroad by trade and diplomacy, and, if necessary, by conquest. The Egyptians exported papyrus, leather, textiles, cereals and dried fish, and in the Empire period exploited the desire of their neighbours for gold, thus maintaining their suzerainty and diplomatic influence. The economic system was based on an annual production and immediate consumption of food, apart from what was husbanded in the State granaries against bad Nile floods. The ruling classes obtained their wealth from personal property, originally given by the king or assigned to them by virtue of the official positions they held in the hierarchy, whether as administrators or priests of the temple estates. They did not capitalize their riches, but stored vases, clothing, jewels and precious metals for their present and future lives, or to leave as legacies for their families.

Trade and commerce were carried out by barter, there being no monetary system, although from about 1580 B.C. articles were given a value in gold, silver and copper, and some fixed weights were in use.

Some years ago a cemetery was discovered at Deir el-Medina on the west bank of the Nile at Thebes, situated between the Valley of the Kings, where the New Kingdom pharaohs were buried, and the funerary temples attached to the royal tombs, which were built on the plain between the desolate mountains of the royal necropolis and the river. Buried in this cemetery were the inhabitants of a nearby village, which was occupied during the New Kingdom period, and the high quality of the workmanship in the tombs is explained by the fact that although the occupants were workmen, they were workmen of a very special kind. They were the masons, sculptors, carpenters and artists who were exclusively employed in building, decorating and repairing the tombs of the kings and queens, and it is not surprising that they turned their skill and talent to their own

Peasants being punished for non-payment of taxes; wall-carving from the tomb of Mereruka

account in building their own tombs. They lived with their families in virtual seclusion from the rest of the working community in this self-contained village, and obviously enjoyed a special status under the administration, proudly calling themselves "Servants in the Place of Truth (Maat)". Their chief held the rank of royal scribe, and they were directly responsible to no less a person than the Vizier. Their houses of sun-baked brick were built in rows of streets, some, belonging to the more important members of the community, being more spacious than others, with the family tomb adjoining, surmounted by a miniature pyramid. They left a large quantity of relics among the rubbish pits and the remains of their houses, chapels and shrines, for they had their own favourite deities and cults, one of the chief being a veneration for the Pharaoh Amenhotpe I of the Eighteenth Dynasty and his Queen Ahmes-Nofretiri, whose tombs their ancestors had doubtless had the privilege of constructing.

They also left an enormous number of papyri and ostraca, the limestone flakes and broken potsherds which, being less expensive than papyrus, were used as writing material. These texts contain lists, legal records and business transactions, which have yielded a wealth of information about their way of living, as well as accounts of family affairs and disputes. They also describe their work in the royal necropolis where they went each day along a track over the hills which is still visible, and along which their resthouses and shrines have been found. The lists give the working hours and shifts of the gangs, and of absentees, and also reveal the wages paid to each grade of worker according to seniority. In short, it is possible to paint a vivid picture of the history, work and personal lives of these individuals with their joys and sorrows, hopes and fears; and while they were probably typical of many such communities engaged on this specially important work, they remained detached from the ordinary villages and had a superior consciousness of their privileged standing as Servants in the Place of Truth.

The writings reveal many personal stories, family relationships and squabbles during several generations, so that it is possible to trace family traits as, for example, that a certain overseer called Peneb was a bad character and up to all kinds of low tricks including the seduction of the wife of one of his colleagues, and that his son was not much better.

One can imagine that the best technical and artistic brains and skills were congregated in this community, and that the inhabitants of Deir el-Medina were of a superior calibre, well endowed with artistic temperament and self-esteem and therefore treated

Painted limestone ostraca from Deir el-Medina

with more than usual tact and indulgence. Among the ostraca were found some delightful "doodles" by some of these artists, scribbled during an idle moment on a stray flake of limestone when, free from the restraint of their official work, they could let their fancy roam in spontaneous thumbnail sketches of one another, a trial sketch or two of the royal features for the tomb they were just then decorating, or with caricatures to amuse their friends.

These workers were independent enough to go on strike, which is more than any other Egyptian worker would have dared to do, when the wages were slow in coming, or for other reasons such as "scandalous happenings in this place of Pharaoh". On one occasion a sit-down strike against the walls of the Ramesseum lasted for several days in spite of negotiations between the workmen and the scribes and priests of the temple whom they urged to appeal to the good lord, the Pharaoh, for immediate payment of their wages of fat, clothes, fish and vegetables for which they had been waiting for eighteen days. After receiving something on account they agreed to go back to work. These strikes of *c.* 1165 B.C. must surely be the earliest on record.

Chapter Seven

DOMESTIC LIFE

There are little or no traces left in Egypt of domestic architecture for, unlike the temples and tombs which were built for eternity, houses were built of perishable materials. It is, however, possible to know what Egyptian houses were like from the illustrations of them in tomb scenes and from tomb models. They were constructed with dried mud-brick, wood or reeds, and as new towns were always built on the same sites as the old, very few foundations remain from which reconstructions can be made, except in the case of one or two sites which were not so re-used, for example, Akhenaten's city at Amarna, the necropolis-workers' village at Deir el-Medina, and some others. From these remaining foundations ground plans have been recovered and models and plans of the general layout of the houses reconstructed. It appears that villages and workmen's dwellings were very similar to those of present-day Egypt: small-roomed, one-storey houses with a terrace facing north to catch the breeze, and a flat roof. Some houses had two floors, while the luxurious villas of the well-to-do stood in walled gardens, in one section of which were situated the kitchens and storerooms, bakeries, butcheries, and granaries. All houses had attached to them conical silos for storing grain, and stalls or stables for the domestic animals. The essential articles of furniture, which of course varied according to wealth, were small stands, stools, and wooden chests and boxes for keeping household stores, pots and dishes, and clothes, while on the walls hung brightly-coloured woven mats. The poorest classes, such as the herdsmen in the marshes, lived in rough shacks made of reeds.

A typical rich man's house in the country during the New Kingdom period would be like a very large bungalow surrounded by a brick wall and a large garden, although his town house would have two and sometimes three storeys. A flight of shallow steps led up to the front door which was flanked by two papyrus columns, and after passing through a porter's lodge and a vestibule the main reception hall was reached. This was long and spacious, the roof gaily painted with geometric designs and supported by painted wooden columns, and lit by painted stone grille windows on one side, the walls decorated with brilliantly coloured designs. The main living-room led out of this hall, and its ceiling was supported by four graceful columns whose capitals were carved as lotus flowers also brightly painted. Clerestory windows high in the walls let in the slanting rays of the sunlight which illuminated the wall paintings of designs of lotus blooms, poppies and cornflowers, interwoven with fruit and duck with heads coloured green and red. The floor was also painted to resemble a pond surrounded by reeds and with lifelike birds and fish. A low brick platform was built along one wall and covered with a rug and cushions, and on it stood the master's chair carved in wood and overlaid with leather, or with inlaid glass or gold and silver leaf. Scattered about the rooms were

One of the beds from the tomb of Tutankhamūn. The footboard is carved with figures of the household god Bes. A head-rest would be placed at the other end

smaller square-shaped chairs and wooden stools inlaid with ivory and ebony, some with straight legs, others with rush seats and crossed legs ending in carved heads of duck or geese, and on the rush-covered floor lay cushions for children and young people to sit on. Opposite the master's dais was another stone platform surrounded by a coping and backed with stone, beside which stood a large jar kept filled with water for ablutions before and after meals – an invariable custom. At sundown in the winter, a shallow pottery pan filled with charcoal was set into the floor in front of the dais to warm the room. A staircase led out of the main room to the roof where the family sometimes slept in hot weather, and a loggia ran along one side of the house, for much time was spent out of doors. The rooms were roofed with palm ribs mixed with mud, laid on rafters decorated with geometric patterns in red, blue, green, and yellow, the rest of the ceiling being whitewashed.

The bedrooms lay at the back of the house, the women's quarters being self-contained and private, no one but the master being allowed to go into them, and their sitting-room was a smaller version of the main living-room. The bed stood on a raised platform round which the walls were thickened to keep out the heat or the cold. The bed had a wooden framework and a linen mesh mattress, the footboard was decorated with carved figures of household deities or other ornamental designs picked out in gold leaf, while the head was furnished with a crescent-shaped head-rest of ivory or wood carved on a stand sometimes formed into a kneeling figure whose outstretched arms supported the crescent.

Adjoining the bedroom was a bathroom consisting of a stone platform on which stood a large spouted vessel for the warm water that was poured over the bather, the idea of washing in static water being repugnant (as it still is among modern Egyptians), the running water carrying the dirt away through a drainage hole into a large pot sunk into the floor. Next to the bathroom was an earth closet with a carved limestone seat. A drainage system as such has never yet been found in Egypt, but the approved

Head-rest found in the tomb of Tutankhamūn, made of hard reddish-brown wood. The central column is carved with the name and titles of the King, and on either side are carved figures of Bes. The carvings were filled in with blue paint

standards of cleanliness must have ensured that some satisfactory arrangements for collection and disposal were made. The Egyptians washed frequently during the day as well as at meal-times, and a basin and spouted jug are often shown beneath dining-tables, a stiff paste with cleansing and lathering ingredients such as ash or fuller's earth being used as soap. Household cleanliness was just as important, and a medical papyrus contains recipes for keeping down household pests: a solution of natron and fish spawn is recommended against insects and fleas, while natron on dried fish placed at the mouth of a snake's hole prevents it from coming out. Oriole fat was probably used to combat flies, an ever prevalent pest in Egypt then as now. The control of rats and mice no doubt encouraged the domestication of the cat; and there were other mixtures used for fumigating clothes, chests, and houses, some of an expensive and exotic kind made from substances which had pleasant scents.

The Egyptians cherished their gardens, and rich and poor alike did their best to maintain one and to grow their own fruit and vegetables. The gardens of the wealthy were shaded by climbing vines, and the straight intersecting paths were lined by date and dôm palms, tamarisks, and many other fruit and flowering trees. In the centre of every garden of any size was a large rectangular pool lined with masonry and well stocked with fish and lotuses. A short flight of steps led down to the pool, and a little boat made of papyrus reeds was kept close by for rowing on the pool in the cool of the evening among the various water-birds which swam on it. Wooden shelters were placed at different points in the garden where large porous earthenware jars were kept filled with drinks and covered with a lid of leaves to keep them cool. The kitchen garden was laid out like the fields, in a criss-cross of square patches with irrigation channels which the gardeners watered with the *shadûf*.

The Egyptian's home was his castle, and the advice of the sage to marry young and found a home and a large family was faithfully followed. While the man was the master of the house, the wife was treated with love and respect, and every consideration was shown her by her husband and the children, who were themselves adored by their parents. "Love your wife", counsels the sage, "fill her stomach, clothe her back; gladden her heart during your lifetime; be not harsh, for gentleness masters her more than strength. Give her what she sighs for, so shall you keep her in your house."

Family ties were strong, and widowed parents and other single relations were absorbed into the household as a matter of course. These traits are characteristic of modern Egyptians, and orphaned nephews and nieces and cousins of all kinds are an obligation cheerfully accepted without question into the family, however straitened a man's circumstances may be. Funerary stelae of married couples often include the whole household of children, relations and friends, servants and household pets, all brought together in eternity.

Women had equal legal and eternal rights with men, and the wife buried with her husband had a place of honour in his tomb, sharing with him the same well-equipped eternal home as she did on earth. They are shown on the tomb walls and on statues in affectionate attitudes, the wife's name generally preceded by the epithets "beloved wife, mistress of the house". The same kind of honour was shown to mothers who sometimes appear in this position in the tomb scenes in front of the wife. Although men had the predominant status in society, they did not tyrannize over their womenfolk. Daughters were loved equally with sons, and though the women lived in separate quarters apart they were not segregated in the Muslim fashion, but came and went freely in the town and countryside. Monogamy was the rule and polygamy the exception; although the wealthy classes kept female slaves as concubines, and if a wife proved sterile it was accepted that a man should take a female serf into his household for the purpose of begetting children who were legally recognized as his heirs and emancipated at his death.

The king was permitted to have more than one wife, and many of the pharaohs had several, only one of whom, the Chief Great Wife, ranked as queen, although the off-spring of other wives were brought up as princes and princesses and had rights of succession, particularly if there lacked a direct male heir. The king kept harems attached to his palaces which were supported by rents and taxes and controlled by a male bureaucracy of directors, scribes, and servants, who were not eunuchs. Here the queens and princesses lived with their ladies and attendants, and here princes from foreign courts, who often came to be brought up with the pharaoh's children as a matter of policy, had their quarters. The idea of a life of idleness and luxury in the harem is belied by the fact that the ladies included in their duties weaving on an industrial scale.

While most careers were closed to women, they served in the temples as minor priestesses, singers, musicians and dancers. Peasant women worked hard in the fields, and at baking, brewing, weaving and spinning among other domestic tasks.

There is nothing to tell us what the marriage ceremony consisted of, if it existed at all, but legal contracts were drawn up confirming the married state, by which two-thirds of the husband's property was bestowed in the wife's name, and the rest of their joint property divided according to a fixed statutory proportion, while the children, male and female, inherited in equal shares. Marriages were arranged by feudal patrons with the parents concerned, and suitable matches were promoted between young people; but there was still a large element of free choice. A suitor took presents to the

The daughters of Amenhotpe III carrying libation vessels at a religious festival. Between each pair are sacrificial jars on wooden stands. Carved relief from a Theban tomb

home of his beloved, and love songs surviving from the New Kingdom indicate a good deal of freedom between young people in love. Probably composed to be sung at banquets, they are remarkable for their delicacy of passion, but it is more than likely that the subtler meanings behind some of the lines and similes escape us: "Her hair is blacker than night, blacker than sloes. Red is her mouth, redder than jasper . . . Would I were her Negress that is her handmaid then would I behold the colour of all her limbs. Would I were the washerman . . . I would wash out the unguents which are in her clothing."

Divorce was recognized, with suitable compensation made to the wife, while adultery in women was punished by burning at the stake, or, less severely, by divorce.

The Egyptians were fond of animals, and monkeys were kept as pets on account of their amusing antics; also the tame Nile goose, perhaps because it was the sacred bird of Amūn, and both were allowed the run of the house. Cats were depicted in the Old Kingdom scenes living wild in the marshes hunting and fishing, but from the Middle Kingdom onwards they appear as house pets along with monkeys and geese. They were a sand-coloured tabby variety, like their present-day descendants which run half wild about the villages, and seem to have fared better in ancient days, sitting on their owners' laps, clawing at their skirts and being fed titbits from their master's table at meal-times (plate 5). This domestic species differs from the indigenous wild cat and seems to have been introduced from outside Egypt. During the Late Period cats were worshipped, and cemeteries of cat mummies date from this period. It was only in late times that animal worship reached a climax: previously animals were deified more by

Left. Bronze statue of a cat with ear-rings. Late Period. *Right.* Servant girl grinding corn; painted limestone model (Dyn. VI)

virtue of their aspects or manifestations of certain powers attributed to the anthropomorphic gods with which they were associated.

Dogs were kept as guardians and for sport, and were often depicted with their masters in tomb scenes, and while from earliest times they seem to have been regarded as man's friend, they do not appear in the house. They were a long-legged greyhound breed, or curly-tailed salukis and basset hounds.

Food was home-produced on the private estates, and large quantities of beef, duck, pigeons, quails and geese were eaten, as well as vegetables and fruit. Bread and cakes and infinite varieties of sweetmeats were made, the chief ingredients being butter and cream, geese' and calves' fat sweetened with honey.

Women were employed to grind the flour, chanting to the rhythm of the laborious task, which was done by hand with a stone in hollow containers consisting of two parts, the flour being ground on the upper part and gathered in the lower part. The dough was then heated in conical moulds and placed in rows on stands and covered over until baked. Later, loaves were baked in earthenware ovens; and at all times flat bread loaves were baked in the hot sand as the Bedouin still do to this day.

The most popular national drink was beer made from wheat or emmer, which seems to have been very similar to *bouza*, a beer drunk in Egypt today and brewed by a method used in Nubia and the Sudan. This method approximates closely to that which must have been used by the ancient Egyptians as depicted on the tomb walls in scenes of brewing. Coarsely ground wheat is kneaded with water into a dough, yeast being added, then lightly baked into thick loaves in order not to destroy the enzymes or kill the yeast. A quarter of the quantity of wheat used, after being moistened with water, is exposed to the air and crushed while still moist. This is then added to the loaves, which have been broken up, and the mixture is put into a vessel and allowed to ferment, after which it is strained through a sieve into jars. The beer was almost certainly not malted, fermentation being caused by the conversion of the natural sugars in the grain into

Wooden model of oxen ploughing

dextrose by one of the enzymes of the yeast; neither were any bitter or other flavouring substances added, as hops are nowadays, except possibly when the beer was used medicinally.

In order to perform all these tasks on the premises, well-to-do people had large numbers of servants and retainers, gardeners and estate workers, butchers, cooks, bakers and brewers. Weaving and spinning were done by women and were confined to linen, wool not being worn until Greek times. The method employed probably goes back to predynastic times, the yarn being spun by hand on a small spindle from which the thread depended. Horizontal hand looms were first used, the vertical type of loom appearing at the time of the Hyksos. Although quantities of loom weights, distaffs, spindles and spindle whorls have been found, no looms have ever come to light. The texture of the linen varies from the coarsest to the finest kind, and there is little difference between the finest linen of ancient Egypt and the best modern fabric.

There are examples of tapestry weaving and embroidery, and in Tutankhamūn's tomb were found his linen gloves trimmed with a tapestry woven design, and an embroidered tunic. As there is no mention of professional tailors or dressmakers it is possible that clothes were made by women in the home.

Cooking consisted mainly of boiling or grilling in earthenware pots on portable cylindrical earthenware stoves with a grill fitted inside to hold the fire and a space below to catch the draught and for collecting the ashes; there were also small metal box ovens with a surface pierced with holes to carry the charcoal or wood fuel. Fire was made by means of a wooden firestick, and no doubt a supply of glowing embers was always kept for kindling.

Egyptians of all ages enjoyed games played on a chequered board with thirty-three squares, the precise rules of which are not known. The moves of the pieces were determined by casting gaming rods. Another well-known game was played on a board shaped like a coiled snake marked off into sections; and in the New Kingdom a popular

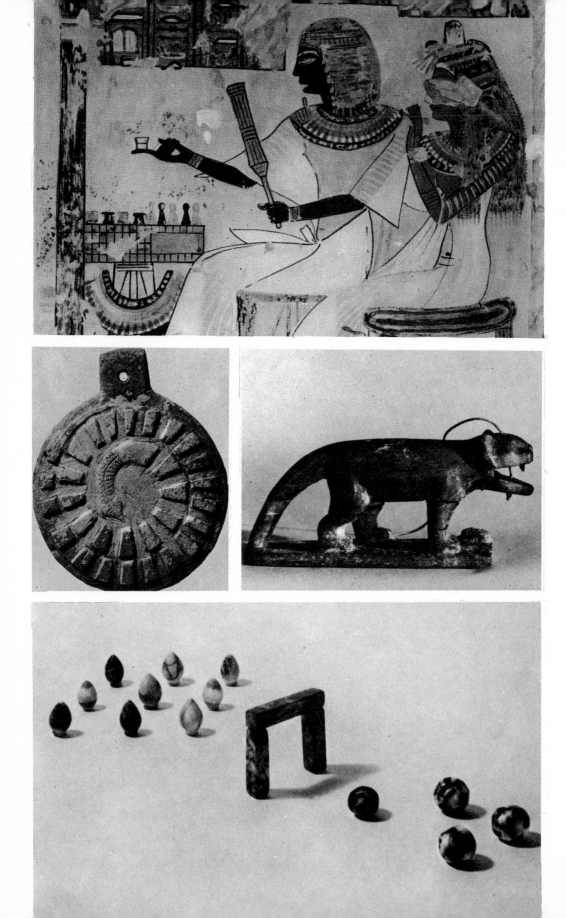

board game was played with five pieces a side, the heads of which were shaped like those of dogs and wolves, and seems to have consisted of beating one's opponent "home", as in Ludo and similar games of the present day.

Children played together in groups, the boys at leap-frog, obstacle races and wrestling; the girls at games of skill such as juggling, dancing and ball games.

Many children's toys have been found buried with their young owners: dolls made of wood or linen with movable arms and legs, toy furniture, wooden tops, and many kinds of toy animals with jaws and limbs that could be worked with a string. A particularly attractive one is the group of dancing pigmies manipulated by strings, a replica of the live pigmies who, particularly in the Old Kingdom, were brought from Nubia to be kept in the household as human pets, and who were highly favoured by their owners.

Fishing and fowling were always popular outdoor sports, and were enjoyed by the whole family. The birds were brought down with a throwstick by the husband, who was accompanied in his graceful reed skiff by his wife and daughters who clapped their hands to scare the birds into the air. A pet cat was sometimes brought along to help catch and retrieve the fallen birds (plate 11).

When fishing for sport, a line and javelin were used, and a tougher sport, when the womenfolk were left behind, was hunting hippopotami and crocodiles by harpooning them with slim javelins from all sides until the great beasts were weak from loss of blood and could be safely hauled to the bank. A more serene pastime was to drop a line into the many backwaters and streams, or into the pool in the garden.

The more serious occupation of fowling to provide stock for the estate and temple farms, where geese and duck of all kinds were kept in yards and reared and hand-fed for the table, or to supply offerings in the temples, was carried out with a claptrap. This consisted of two oblong nets on wooden frames placed side by side in a clearing and kept taut by sticks at each end, roped firmly into the ground and held by a single rope at one end which has hidden under cover of the reeds. Here the men waited in silence until enough birds had wandered into the clearing. At a signal from one man the others pulled hard on the rope, the net turned over on its wooden edges and closed over the birds. They were then transferred into cages and carried alive to the yards or to the market where they were sold in exchange for other commodities such as bread, linen, pottery or other kinds of food.

Fish formed a large part of the diet among the poorer classes and the occupational fishermen used drag-nets to catch the fish which were brought to shore, slit, salted and hung in the sun to dry.

Royal palaces, like other domestic architecture, were built of wood and brick so that only the most pitiful remains are left, and only the most patient and scholarly reconstruction enables us to visualize their extent and beauty. It has been possible to reconstruct on paper Akhenaten's palace at Amarna from the foundations; and the remains of the palace of his father, Amenhotpe III, at Malkata near Thebes enable some idea to be formed of the vast area covered by these edifices of the New Kingdom. There were numbers of state and private apartments for the king and his queens and harem ladies, and a complex of subsidiary buildings for kitchens, storerooms, and wine cellars, and a great number of open courts for the reception of state officials and foreign emissaries. A feature of the palaces was a Window of Appearances where the king

Top left. A man and his wife playing a board game resembling draughts; painted scene from a New Kingdom tomb. *Centre left.* Predynastic model of the game of "serpent" and toy cat with movable jaw. *Left.* Predynastic model of the game of ninepins

appeared before the populace and dispensed rewards and decorations to his courtiers and favoured servants to the acclamations of the crowd. Scenes of this kind are found carved on the tomb-walls of the recipients of these royal favours.

The interior decorations of these palaces must have been sumptuous to a degree, with wall paintings and decorations of the highest quality; and the furniture found in Tutankhamūn's and other royal tombs conveys some notion of the luxury with which they were equipped.

It is only to be expected that in the course of three thousand years fashions in dress and hair styles should vary and show a tendency to become more elaborate as time went on and as distinctions between people and their personal taste became more varied and sophisticated; yet, generally speaking, the unvarying climate tended to keep dress simple and light, and basically it remained fairly constant. The simple styles of the Old Kingdom, a linen loin-cloth or short apron or skirt for men knotted at the waist, with sometimes a sleeveless tunic, and a straight linen tunic for women supported by crossed straps under the breasts (plate 9), was universally worn by kings and queens and commoners alike. In the New Kingdom the upper classes of both sexes wore more flowing garments with sleeved tunics and cloaks, often finely pleated, still of very fine white linen, colour being provided by elaborate jewelled collars, necklaces, bracelets, pectorals and ear-rings.

Left. Carved wooden figures wearing the finely pleated dress and elaborate wigs of the New Kingdom period. *Right*. Detail from the carved limestone sarcophagus of Kawit, a lady of the Eleventh Dynasty, at her toilet

Men in the Old Kingdom wore their hair short, and women sometimes followed the same style with shoulder-length hair, but more often they wore it long. These styles were replaced in later periods by intricately curled and plaited coiffures; the upper classes wore wigs made of human hair and vegetable fibres, and those worn on ceremonial occasions were dressed in a variety of elaborate ways and further ornamented with diadems, coronets, flowers and jewels. Great trouble was taken over hairdressing by men and women alike, and an array of perfumed ointments, dressings and fixatives were used, and there are many recipes for combating grey hair and baldness. Wigs and wig boxes were buried in the tombs together with other personal possessions deemed essential for eternity.

Open sandals were made of plaited papyrus or reed and prettily ornamented; some were of gold, and may have been worn only on ceremonial occasions, carried by sandal-bearers, to be put on at the appropriate moment. Egyptians seemed just as happy walking about barefoot.

Children presented no great problem where dress was concerned: they went about naked for the first few years, after which the boys were given a loin-cloth and girls a belt or a simple tunic. They wore their hair short except for one curled sidelock hanging over one ear.

Men and women spent a lot of time over their toilet and were attended each morning

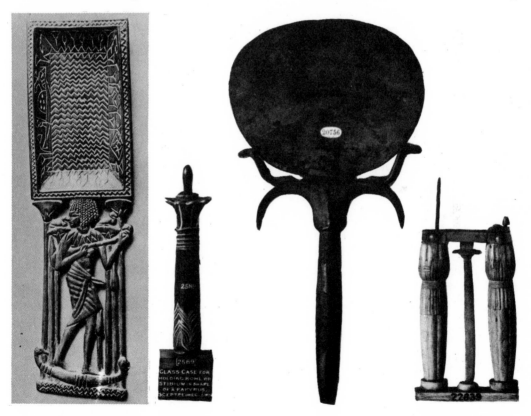

Left. Cosmetic spoon, the bowl decorated in the form of a lake. *Right.* Toilet articles: a container for eye-paint, a mirror, and a double container for eye-paint and the rod with which it was applied

Wooden cosmetic spoon in the form of a girl supporting a duck

by their barbers, manicurists, pedicurists, masseurs and hairdressers, equipped with hooked razors with curved bronze blades, and sets of knives, scrapers, files and tweezers of copper and bronze, and other small implements kept in fitted boxes or leather cases. The poorer sections of the population queued for the attention of the barber in the open, under the trees.

A wide range of cosmetics and beauty preparations was used by both sexes: scented oils and fats for massaging the body in hot weather; cleansing creams consisting of animal or vegetable oils and lime, and perhaps chalk, for restoring youth, and eradicating wrinkles and blemishes. Women painted their cheeks with rouge, and the red pigment found in cosmetic jars is a red ochre which was probably used with a base of vegetable or tallow grease, with perhaps a little gum-resin, and this may be the cosmetic that was also used as lip rouge.

Eye make-up was used from the very earliest period, for which a preparation of green malachite (a green ore of copper) was the earliest and remained the chief one used; the other, which came into use much later and survived into the Coptic period, was of galena (a dark grey ore of lead). The finely ground material was made into a paste or powder, and has been found in the tombs among personal belongings contained in segments of hollow reeds or in small vases, themselves sometimes reed-shaped. The present-day Egyptian *kohl*, which is still extensively used as an eye cosmetic, consists of soot or a mixture of galena and lamp black, and is applied with a small rod made of wood, bone, ivory or metal, which is moistened with water and dipped into the powdered preparation. The ancient Egyptians applied their malachite and galena eye-paint with similar sticks, or with the finger, to add lustre to their naturally almond-shaped eyes, and as a protection against the dust and the glare of the sun, or to ward off flies and other insects.

Chapter Eight

WRITING AND LITERATURE

Education in the accepted sense of the word was confined to the upper strata of Egyptian society, the artisan or craftsman's son being taught his father's trade at home. There were schools attached to the departments of the State administration to which boys were apprenticed at a very early age. A more classical education was provided in the "House of Life", attached to the temple for those whose aim was to pursue a career in the higher reaches of the royal service; and there they received instruction in scientific subjects and in the rituals and textual lore of the religious cult in addition to the basic study of reading and writing.

A boy's first lessons were learnt at home in the form of parental advice and admonition, based largely upon the traditional wisdom literature, which included, as well as moral precepts, practical advice on how to make a good impression by observing the behaviour acceptable in well-bred society. Great stress was laid on not speaking out of turn, or only when one had something worth saying, and in not addressing a superior before being addressed. Table manners were also important, and while it was considered polite to "take that which is set before you" and not to look closely at other people's helpings, it was more polite to eat too much if your host was a greedy man than to embarrass him by eating less than he. "If you sit with many persons, hold the food in abhorrence even if you desire it; it takes only a brief moment to master oneself . . . a cup of water quenches the thirst . . . just a little takes the place of much. He is a miserable man that is greedy for his body . . ."

Other maxims exhort a man "not to be proud because you are a learned man. Seek advice from the ignorant as well as with the wise man", and "do right so long as you live on earth". Children were taught to honour and love their parents especially when they grew old, to be a "staff of old age" to their fathers, and "never to forget what your mother has done for you, repay her for all her care for you. Give her as much bread as she needs and carry her as she carried you, for you were a heavy burden to her".

Reading and writing were taught in the schools by copying, dictation, and chanting aloud to commit to memory the traditional and classical texts and literature, just as the Koran is chanted in Islamic schools in Egypt today, this knowledge being an essential equipment of a well-educated man. Discipline in the schools was strict, if we are to believe the exhortations of the teachers:

"O scribe, be not idle, else you shall be promptly curbed. Do not give your heart to pleasure or you shall be a failure. Write with your hand, read with your mouth, and take advice of those who know more than you . . . a boy's ear is indeed upon his back, and he hearkens to the beating of it . . . do not slacken. Write!" After bewailing the fact that his beatings seem to have little effect, this exasperated tutor goes on: "My heart is sick from speaking advice . . . I shall give you a hundred blows and you will disregard them all." He perseveres, however, with his idle pupil. "I will make a man of you yet, you naughty lad,"

There is no indication that girls went to school, and it is doubtful whether more than a few learned to read and write. Their education was probably confined to domestic matters and artistic accomplishments like music and dancing, and was received at home.

A society in which everything was delegated from a centralized administration necessitated meticulous recording of every conceivable matter and transaction for every aspect of life and resulted in a vast bureaucracy of scribes from the highest to the lowest grades. There were scribes of accounts, of the treasury, of taxes, of the army, and of every department of agriculture down to the humblest type of "civil service" clerks. Equipped with the knowledge of writing and reading, the scribes had almost limitless prospects of advancement, and in a predominantly illiterate community it is little wonder that they regarded themselves as a superior caste and no doubt exploited their position to impress humbler people. It is still the practice in modern Egyptian towns and villages for the peasant to pay a scribe to write his letters for him, as was undoubtedly the case in ancient Egypt.

The scribe boasted that his was "the foremost of professions" and wrote satirical accounts comparing his superior lot with those in other walks of life. "The scribe lands at the river-bank to collect the tax and says 'give corn!' and beats the peasant furiously if owing to a bad harvest he is unable to pay." "He is bound and thrown into the well. He is soused in a headlong dipping. But a scribe, he is a controller of everyone. He who works in writing is not taxed, he has no dues to pay. Take note of this." In a letter to a student a chief record-keeper of Pharaoh has this to say. "Be a scribe. It saves you from toil and protects you from all manner of work", and he compares his lot with that of a soldier or a groom. Such a man while still a boy will merely run errands or be put to work in the fields, and if he stops work for an instant his livelihood stops. As to the baker, "he regularly bakes and puts bread on to the fire; his head is inside the oven whilst his son holds fast his feet. In the event of slipping from his son's hand he thereby falls down into the oven's bottom. Look for yourself with your own eye. The professions are set before you. The washerman spends the whole day going up and down, all of him is weak through whitening the clothes of his neighbours every day and washing their linen. The potter is smeared with earth . . . his hands and feet are full of clay, he is like one who is in the mire." But a scribe owns a horse and chariot, he has a boat on the Nile and a villa in the city; he is a "trusty one of the King attired in fine clothes".

Apart from this typical arrogance displayed by a complacent group of educated men in an ignorant community the title of scribe conveyed the status-symbol of a real intellectual fraternity and was assumed by the highest in the land, including royal princes, who often had themselves depicted as scribes in their statues. It is possible that the title of "scribe" carried with it some connotation of scholarly learning equivalent to a degree of Doctor of Letters for those of whom it could be said that "the lore of books is graven on your heart".

The scribe's equipment consisted of a brush made from a rush stem, the end being cut at a slant and chewed to make a fine point, and he would carry spare brushes tucked

Plate 11. Fowling in the papyrus marshes: a scene from the tomb of Nebamun, a scribe of the Eighteenth Dynasty
Overleaf Plate 12. The second coffin of Tutankhamūn, made of wood covered with gold foil inlaid with coloured opaque glass and faience

behind his ear. A palette made of wood or ivory for mixing the inks served also as a pen-case with slots at one end with a sliding lid to hold the brushes when not in use. Black and red inks, mixed with gum and water, were used and when dry were fixed on to the palette in small solid blocks, or fitted into cavities in the palette; a shoulder-sack containing the rolls of papyrus and a small pot for water to mix the colours completed the outfit except for a damp rag or a pointed piece of sandstone for erasing mistakes. The palettes were often carved with the owner's name and with a prayer to Thoth, the god of writing and scribes.

Details of the manufacture of papyrus are not illustrated in paintings and reliefs or even described in the texts, and the accounts left by the Greeks have not been proved accurate. An experiment was made in 1948 with fresh papyrus, which had been specially grown in a private garden near Cairo, which yielded a thin paper with a suitable surface for writing. The method used was to cut a number of sections of the green stem into lengths that could be easily manipulated. The outer rind was stripped off and the inner pith cut into thicker slices, not necessarily all of the same thickness. An absorbent cloth was placed on a table, and a number of the slices of the pith arranged on it parallel to, and slightly overlapping, one another. A second layer was placed across the first, also slightly overlapping, then covered with another thin absorbent cloth, and the whole beaten for an hour or two with a wooden mallet. Finally the material was placed in a small press for several hours, after which the slices became welded together, adhering firmly to one another.

Sheets of papyrus were anything up to eight or nine yards in length and were carried and stored in rolls tied round the middle with a red cord. The scribe wrote standing up when the papyrus was small, but when a large sheet was used he sat on the ground, holding the roll in his left hand while he unrolled from one end as much as he needed and laid it flat on his lap (plate 15). When he had filled the page he unrolled another section, and so on until the end of the roll was reached. Papyrus being an expensive commodity, both sides were used and often re-used many times, so that the text on one side may bear no relation to that on the reverse. Normally the scribe wrote from right to left in vertical columns, but from the Middle Kingdom writing in horizontal lines appears which evidently became universal, a change in practice probably due to the danger of smudging a newly-written column while writing the next.

Hieroglyphic is the name given by the Greeks to the signs which they found carved on the walls of the temples and tombs, on statues and on coffins. It means literally "sacred writing" and was so called because by the time the Greeks came to Egypt this script was used exclusively for religious and ceremonial texts, although originally it was in common use for everyday purposes as well. The hieroglyphic writing was fully developed at a very early date, and had its origins in "picture-writing", the earliest stage of many primitive scripts, where a picture is drawn of an object which is instantly recognizable. These ideograms came to represent abstract ideas and other subjects which had the same sound but which could not be pictorially represented, thus acquiring a phonetic value. For example, a word like "belief" which has no visible quality can be written with pictures of a bee and a leaf, in which case these objects are regarded as phonograms, on the principle of the rebus or charade. Another example is the city of Oxford as the Egyptians might have written it: the coat of arms of the city

Plate 13. Tutankhamūn's fan, made of wood covered with sheet gold, depicting Pharaoh hunting ostriches in the desert

101

Plate 14. Ornamental casket from the tomb of Tutankhamūn, made of coniferous wood and ivory. The hieroglyphic inscriptions are filled with black pigment and represent the names and titles of the King and Queen

Top left. Wood relief from the mastaba of Hesirē, an official of King Djoser. He is seated at an offering-table, holding the staff and wand of his rank, and has a scribe's outfit slung over his shoulder. *Top right*. Statuette of a priest and scribe of the god Thoth, whom he carries on his shoulders in the form of an ape. New Kingdom. *Above*. A scribe's palette is an ox upon a representation of water, and this picture on road signs, etc. immediately conveys the idea of the city, and not of an ox or a ford. A further development took place when the hieroglyphic signs came to stand for individual consonants, and it was when this fact was realised by the early decipherers that the key to the reading of the script was found.

The hieroglyphs were carefully and often beautifully carved and painted, and were used as much for their decorative effect as for conveying information, but as writing became used more and more for administrative and practical purposes a cursive form of hieroglyphs came into use as a result of writing with a rush pen on papyrus. From this developed the hieratic script, the signs at first being not much different from the hieroglyphic forms except that they were often abbreviated. In course of time the hieratic characters acquired distinctive outlines of their own, and bear a somewhat similar relationship to hieroglyphs as that of handwriting to printing.

The hieratic script developed in its turn over a period of time into the latest form of Egyptian writing, demotic, a rapid and degenerate form of hieratic in which it is very difficult to recognize the original hieroglyphic forms, and which is also very difficult to read. Demotic was in common use from about the eighth century B.C. until late Roman times. This "popular" script was used for business and legal documents and for the literary writings of the period. Hieroglyphic and hieratic were used contemporaneously, but hieroglyphic became more and more reserved for religious and ceremonial texts so that eventually it was understood only by the priests and temple scribes.

The Egyptian language survived in Coptic and was written with the Greek alphabet to which were added seven characters taken from the demotic script, and this was the language spoken by the Christian descendants of the ancient Egyptians. It still survives in the liturgy of the Coptic Church, just as Latin has been used in the Roman Catholic Church. The importance of Coptic in deciphering the hieroglyphs is obvious, and it was through the study of this old half-forgotten tongue that the efforts of the early scholars who tackled the problem of decipherment met with success.

Three names will always be associated with the great discovery which led to the understanding of the hieroglyphs: those of Dr Thomas Young, a famous English physicist and a student of oriental languages, and Jean François Champollion, a French oriental scholar, and of the famous Rosetta Stone, although other monuments had been studied by scholars whose efforts paved the way towards the final discovery.

The Rosetta Stone is a large slab of black basalt which was found in 1799, when Egypt was under French occupation, by an officer serving in Napoleon's army while strengthening a fort in the Western Delta near the town of Rosetta. It eventually came into the possession of the British Museum in 1802 where it still is. It was a decree set up in 196 B.C. by Ptolemy V, one of the Greek kings of Egypt, and was carved in two languages and three scripts: hieroglyphic, demotic and Greek. It was easy enough to translate the Greek portion of the text; the demotic part was then studied by various scholars. It had been recognized that in hieroglyphic royal names were written in cartouches, the French word for "ring" or "shield": ⬭. It was therefore decided to tackle the royal names first, and it was clear that such cartouches occurred where the name of Ptolemy appeared in the Greek text. Dr Young was responsible for confirming that the cartouches contained royal names and that the demotic and hieroglyphic writing

were closely related; but it was Champollion who succeeded in deciphering the names Ptolemy and Cleopatra on the Rosetta Stone. Since they contained identical letters having the same phonetic value, P, T, and L, and were written alike in Greek and demotic, it was reasonable to suppose that where these sounds occurred in the hieroglyphic version of the names the same signs would be used in each. This proved to be the case, for the letter P in both names was found to be written with the same sign ▢ where P occurred:

(A) Ptolemy

(B) Cleopatra

Champollion saw that number 1 in (A) and number 5 in (B) are identical, so they must be the letter P; number 4 in (A) and number 2 in (B) are also the same, and so must represent the letter L. Sign number 1 in (B) must be K, and it does not occur in the name Ptolemy (A).

In Cleopatra's cartouche the value of three signs had been obtained.

In the Greek form of the name there are two vowels between CL and P, so numbers 3 and 4 must represent E and O. Since T follows P in Ptolemy, and there is a T in Cleopatra, it was assumed, correctly, that ⌒ and ⌒ (Nos 2 in (A), and 7 in (B)) in hieroglyphic had more or less the same sound value. The two signs numbered 6 and 9 are in the place of the two A's in Cleopatra, so 𓅓 must have the value of A. This now gave:

Number 8 obviously stood for R leaving only the two end signs and these, as Young had previously noted, always followed the name of a goddess or a queen, and were correctly assumed to be a feminine ending. Comparing what had been deciphered in Cleopatra's name with that of Ptolemy:

it followed that numbers 5 and 6 must be M and Y, and number 7 S, conforming with the Greek spelling Ptolemaios.

It was Champollion's genius which developed this method and, by his brilliant work, he established the correct method of reading the hieroglyphs so that before he died at a very early age in 1832 he had correctly read the names and titles of most of the Roman emperors of Egypt, and many other texts besides. He drew up a list of hieroglyphs and formulated a grammar of the language which formed the basis upon which succeeding generations of Egyptologists have brought the knowledge of the Egyptian language to its present high level.

It will always remain a mystery, however, how the language was pronounced, since

Top left. Examples of Egyptian hieroglyphs; painted, carved, and written with a rush pen on papyrus. *Centre left*. Part of the story of the Eloquent Peasant, written in hieratic script on papyrus. *Left*. The Rosetta Stone

no vowels were written and only the consonantal skeletons of words can be read. The vowels, however, survived in Coptic, which has made it possible to reconstruct some words and names with some approximation to the original pronunciation. The Egyptians themselves must have experienced the same difficulty in recognizing the meaning of different words having the same consonants, and they added determinative signs as a clue to the word's meaning. There are over a hundred of these determinatives, some of the more obvious being the figure of a man, woman or child for words with male and female meanings and those connected with youth; or of a man holding a stick for words conveying any energetic or violent action. A sun is added to words denoting light, or time of day; a sparrow, one of the pests of the fields, denoting anything mean or bad. A picture of the scribe's outfit was used as a determinative for words connected with writing or learning of any kind.

Armed with this knowledge, it has been possible for Egyptologists to probe into the literature of the Egyptians, which by its quantity and quality is unique in pre-classical times, and from which many traditional forms have derived. It is mainly written in hieratic on papyrus rolls, wooden tablets, and ostraca, and, fragmentary though many of these survivals are, their variety and content demonstrate the richness and extent of the literature. The most popular, and therefore the most frequently copied throughout Egyptian history, were the narratives of adventures and stories which constituted a veritable folklore in which the doings of historical kings and famous men are recounted, well laced with magical imagery based on ancient myths and events in the lives of the archaic gods and goddesses.

Probably the most highly esteemed of all were the Wisdom Texts, many of which date from the days of the Old Kingdom; they were attributed to wise men of old like Imhotep, Djoser's architect, and were written in the form of an instruction by a father to his son. In fact, they took the place of religious teaching in moral education from generation to generation. They contain a fund of sound precepts based on tradition and worldly experience, and display a remarkable degree of humanity, circumspection and excellent advice for restraint in speech and action, and decent conduct towards one's fellow men, and are amplified by much sagacious advice on worldly advancement. The importance of good manners and observance of the correct etiquette in all situations of daily life are also stressed.

The teachings of one New Kingdom sage contain several maxims which are recognizable in the Book of Proverbs, which they obviously inspired. Egypt's early and continuous contact with the Near East must have disseminated many Egyptian tales through the oriental love of listening to the story-teller in the market-place; so much so that common elements in Egyptian stories – of travellers' tales, of shipwrecked sailors on magic islands peopled with friendly monsters who talk in human language and who turn out to be benignant deities, of magical transformation of humans into flowers or animals, of prophecies and erring wives – can be traced in the Greek romances and have faint echoes in popular tales the world over.

Chapter Nine

MORALITY AND ETHICS

It is obviously impossible at this distance of time to understand the inner workings of the Egyptain mind and to assess their real attitude to right and wrong. In spite of the scholars' not inconsiderable knowledge of the language, the subtler definitions escape them, and translations, however literal, tend to be coloured with shades of meaning supplied by our own mental attitude which is quite incompatible with that of an archaic oriental civilization. The best that can be attempted in assessing how the individual conscience of an Egyptian reacted is to take at its face value the accepted view of the society in which he lived, and which is expressed in the didactic literature which was taught in the schools and written, not by priests as religious teaching, but by sages and sometimes by wise and good kings, and revered as the accumulated wisdom of the ages. Much also can be gleaned from the epitaphs of those who wished their memory to be held in high esteem by posterity.

From these sources it can be assumed that there was no distinction between intellectual and purely moral qualities. Virtue was not always its own reward, but the observance of the ethical code resulted in worldly profit and advancement, a long life, and a "goodly burial in the west". Whether or not it was lived up to, it demonstrates a code of conduct and precept which, whatever the motive, would be acceptable today, and was admirable in an archaic society of so remote an epoch. It demanded first and foremost obedience and love of Maat in the person of the king and the gods, observation of the ritual, and consideration for one's neighbour. Decorous behaviour, including the right manner of address to one's superiors, control over one's tongue and a good expression of language, proper deportment, and acceptable table manners, were all part and parcel of leading a good life. The ideal is indicated by the qualities inscribed on the tomb stelae of private people and presumed to be possessed in abundance by the owner: "I was one loved by his father, praised by his mother, and esteemed by his friends and his city and by all who knew him" and, above all, "the object of tender affection in the heart of the King, loving Maat, holding evil in abhorrence". As "evil" consisted of all that conflicted with the right order, and "good" meant the upholding of that order in everything, the fusion of material benefits with what we would call "spiritual" virtue may not be so contradictory as might appear. However, a certain amount of mysticism seems to have gone with this idea: the heart, not the brain, was considered to be the seat of intelligence and will, and some idea of inspiration from within appears to have existed. "The heart enriches the character", they maintained, "it is the powerful master for creating good"; and there is evidence of personal devotion to their chosen deities and cults for their own sake by ordinary individuals who found consolation in this and in repenting their misdeeds.

A common chapter included in the papyri forming the "Book of the Dead" which was placed in the tomb with the deceased was that of the "weighing of the heart", the seat of intelligence and will (plate 16). It points to some idea of judgment after death, and is illuminating in demonstrating what was considered the right conduct through life. Osiris, as supreme judge of the dead, surrounded by forty-two other gods, sits in a judgment hall, while the deceased man or woman is led before him by Anubis, the protector of the dead, and his heart is placed in a balance opposite Maat, the goddess of Truth represented by a feather, the hieroglyphic sign used in writing her name. Thoth, the god of writing and wisdom, records the results while the deceased recites the formula denying his guilt against the accepted moral law: "I have committed no injustice against men, I have not maltreated animals, I have not killed anyone . . . I did not deny bread to the hungry, or drink to the thirsty, or neglect to console the widow and orphan. . . ." A lengthy catalogue follows, revealing in its ethical content. This "negative confession" is duly recorded by Thoth and if, by the magic power of its faultless recitation, the heart remains equally balanced with Maat, the judges are satisfied and the dead person is admitted into the kingdom of Osiris.

There is no record of any judgement ever going against the deceased, or of his seizure by the monstrous animal waiting for those found wanting. The efficacy of the proper recital is all that is required, and brings in the magical element which appears to be inherent in all Egyptian religious and moral thought and thereby renders it impossible to grasp in its true significance.

In this connection it is the multiplicity of gods in ancient Egypt which seems incomprehensible to us, but which may have arisen partly from the people's conservative character. The original nomadic tribes of the Nile Valley each had their own tribal cult personified by some animal, natural object, or fetish which became their standard. After unification, and with the growth of settled communities and towns, these gods each became the deity attached to some particular locality or region, and their cults remained in spite of the later accretion of other national gods. As new ideas developed, such as the sun religion of Rē at Heliopolis, or the political ascendancy of Amūn at Thebes, the national gods became fused with the local cults, none of which was discarded. The Egyptians apparently did not think it strange to worship multiple aspects of the same god, but simply added the attributes and names of new gods to the old. They saw in them, perhaps, different aspects of the same supreme deity, not entirely inconsistent with a monotheistic tendency. In the more intellectual writings "god" is often referred to without a specific name as a universal power, and in one Old Kingdom text it is said that "it is not the will of man which is realized, but the plan of god".

Chapter Ten

LAW AND JUSTICE

In theory all classes of Egyptians were equal in the sight of the civil law, and were equally subject to the effects of royal decrees issued by the king and inscribed on stelae and set up in the temples throughout Egypt; but it is equally clear that all classes of citizens did not share the same legal rights in inheritance and suchlike matters. There exists an abundance of contracts between individuals, deeds duly witnessed and officially sealed, and testimonies on oath dealing with a variety of matters such as the transference of property, contesting of wills, and so on; but the niceties of the legal phraseology is extremely difficult to translate into intelligible terms and much remains obscure concerning the details of a society so remote in time from our own.

The code relating to the dispensation of justice was very strictly laid down in the instructions to the Vizier formally given to him by the king when investing him in the high office of Chief Justice. He was exhorted to show no fear or favour, and to make himself available to receive and listen to all classes of petitioners with sympathy, patience and an open mind. Numerous local councils, composed of the city's notables, existed up and down the country to deal with minor cases and disputes which were heard on the spot. The proceedings were interminable, since the litigants presented their own cases, and the more verbiage they indulged in the more chance there was of success. The Egyptians' love of high-flown language for its own sake, and the apparently universal right of appeal by high and low, are both illustrated in a popular classic story dating from the First Intermediate Period and retold and recopied in later periods in the schools as a model of rhetoric. It concerns a peasant from one of the oases leading his donkey laden with the produce of his plot to market in the nearest town who by a trick was robbed of his donkey and his goods on the way. The peasant brought his complaint to the nomarch of the province in which the unhappy event took place, and his eloquence in pleading his case so delighted the court that they detained him for months with objections and indecisive arguments simply in order to goad him on to further flights of eloquence, and in order to record his vivid accusations and appeals and send them to the King for his delectation and entertainment. They finally had the grace to decide in his favour, and to recompense him handsomely for his sufferings.

Crimes against the State or the king's person were dealt with by special courts, and intervention by the sovereign himself is known in certain cases of conspiracy in the harem by minor queens to place their own sons on the throne, or of plots to assassinate the king. The punishments meted out to criminals ranged from beating with a stick, in accordance with a carefully graded scale in proportion to the offence, to cutting off the nose or ears or both, and deportation to the stone quarries and mines. The death penalty was reserved for rebellion and for adultery by women, and consisted of beheading, burning, and voluntary suicide for highly placed dignitaries. Those condemned to forced labour in the mines or on irrigation and field work were detained in the many impregnable fortresses near the frontiers.

A famous case, which had a sequel in the nineteenth century A.D., was in connection with the tomb robberies which took place in the time of Ramesses IX, a troubled period of economic instability, when gangs of desperate men sought to alleviate their poverty by systematic robbery of the rich treasure known to be buried in the private and royal tombs in the Theban hills. Pillaging of tombs had been going on for centuries, but never to the organized extent reached at this time. There is no doubt that officials of the temples and the necropolis were involved, if only because of their inside knowledge of the whereabouts and entrances of the royal tombs, which were constructed in secret "no one seeing, no one knowing". Obviously, in such large undertakings leakages of information were bound to occur, and bribery has always been a feature of oriental life. In the event, it was the rivalries between officials on the east and west banks of the Nile at Thebes that led one to betray the other, and the papyrus which records the trial of the accused demonstrates a confusion of confessions by some, and assertions by others that all was well in the necropolis. The robberies did not stop, however, and during the following dynasty of priest-kings of Amūn, a thorough investigation was carried out in the royal tombs, the mummies were restored, and the tombs were re-sealed. Some of the royal mummies were removed and re-buried in other tombs and hiding places in the Theban hills. The most famous pharaohs of the New Kingdom, Tuthmosis III, Sety I, Ramesses II, and others, together with what treasures were left from the depredations of the robbers, were all transferred to a secret tomb excavated near Deir el-Bahri where they lay for 3,000 years.

In the latter half of the nineteenth century A.D., the steady appearance in the antiquity dealers' shops in Cairo of exceptionally rich and hitherto unrecorded treasures which could only be attributed to royalty aroused suspicion, and investigations led to the Luxor village of el-Qurna where it was found that a family called el-Rashid had recently become very prosperous. It seemed that the donkey of one of them, in scrabbling the sand at the foot of a cliff, had unwittingly unearthed the entrance to the deep cache where the priest-kings of the Twenty-First Dynasty had re-buried the royal mummies more than three thousand years earlier. Thereafter the el-Rashid family and their fellow tomb-robbers possessed an unlimited bank account on which they proceeded to draw until suspicion lighted on them. All the interrogations by the local magistrate could not elicit any information or admissions, even when methods resembling those of their ancestors were resorted to. Finally, history repeated itself, and the thieves fell out among themselves and gave each other away. The parallel did not stop there: in July 1881 the Antiquities Service in Cairo removed the treasure and the royal mummies to the Cairo Museum and conveyed them thither by boat from Luxor. All the way along the Nile, peasant women on both banks followed the boat wailing and tearing their hair like the mourning women of old. The conscientious scribe at the customs house in Cairo demanded a tax on dutiable freight brought up by river. The tax list did not include the duty to be levied on dead pharaohs, so the scribe, not to be deprived of his great moment of authority, decided that the appropriate tax should be that levied on dried fish.

The mummified head of Sety I

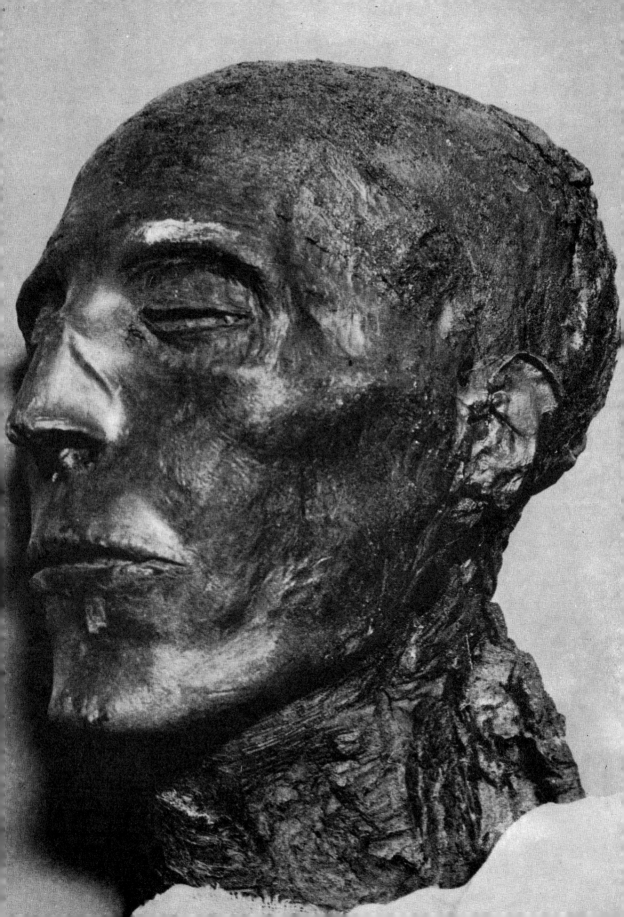

Chapter Eleven

SCIENCE

The tradition that attributes to the ancient Egyptians an extraordinary degree of scientific knowledge and philosophical wisdom is not borne out by the increasingly accurate assessment of existing archaeological and textual evidence. Their admitted capacity for dealing with any technical problems that arose in the pursuance of their many-sided activities and sophisticated needs did not go much beyond their practical solution. For utilitarian purposes they knew how to measure the land and the Nile waters, and devised the necessary means for doing so. They also made precise and intelligent observations in the fields of astronomy, medicine and botany, but further study into the purely intellectual realms of these subjects did not interest them, and knowledge for its own sake without practical application did not appeal to these materially-minded people.

From what can be gleaned from the few mathematical documents which survive, there was a written numerical system from 1 to 1,000,000 and they were able to add, subtract, divide and multiply. Simple fractions were conceived with only one enumerator, and were expressed by using the word meaning "part" below which was written the denominator. There were special words for $\frac{1}{2}$ and $\frac{1}{4}$; while $\frac{2}{3}$ and $\frac{3}{4}$ were expressed by a sign meaning "the two parts" (out of three), and "the three parts" (out of four). The chief linear measurements which can be identified were the royal cubit (about 20·62 inches, and equal to seven palms (of the hand), or twenty-eight fingers), and the short cubit (about 17·72 inches). A "river-measure", corresponding with the Greek *schoinos* (about 20,000 cubits) was used for measuring long areas. Some measures of capacity have been approximated to the bushel and half-litre.

Geometry was required for measuring fields or the volume of buildings and pyramids, and they possessed sufficient knowledge for this purpose which, while seeming somewhat clumsy, corresponds to the correct formulae. It is doubtful whether they had any knowledge of algebra, this being an invention of the Babylonians.

Pure mathematics evidently did not appeal to the Egyptians, and it was left to the Babylonians and the Greeks to develop this science, for which, however, Egypt undoubtedly paved the way. Nevertheless, the occurrence at the end of some calculations, only roughly comparable with proofs, of the phrase "it is equal", or "it is just that", i.e. Q.E.D., indicates that they had some aspirations in the direction of pure mathematical thought.

Another fallacy which credits the Egyptians with being deeply versed in astrology is probably due to the development, during the years preceding and following the rise of Christianity, of Hellenistic and Mesopotamian creeds and doctrines in Alexandria, at that time the centre of learning where the intelligentsia and savants of the eastern world congregated and imported this and other ideas. The Egyptians' ancient and deep-rooted belief in lucky and unlucky days by which they cast personal horoscopes is something quite different, and was based on mythological events and occasions in the life-stories of their own gods and goddesses. This kind of superstition was prevalent at all times, and the first thing a father did on the birth of his child was to discover what its destiny in life was to be, and to decide how best to name it to ensure its good fortune, if this was predicted, or to avoid the results of an unlucky verdict.

In astronomy, on the other hand, the Egyptians were quite advanced, their observations being precise enough to compile charts of the heavens and tables of the movements of celestial bodies which were carved in relief on the ceilings of tombs and temples. The accuracy of their observations is attested by the division of the calendar, and by the distinctions which were made between planets, "the stars which have no rest", and the fixed stars, which were sometimes associated with the dead who were said to have become "imperishable stars".

Day and night were divided into twelve hours each which were unequal in length according to the season, the night hours being shorter in the summer than in winter. It was the Hellenistic peoples who invented the division of the hour into sixty minutes following the Babylonian sexagesimal system. The Egyptians relied on sun-dials and clepsydra (water-clocks) to tell the time during the daylight hours; at night they relied on the decan stars, and had drawn up tables of the positions of these constellations and their appearance in the sky. During an approximate ten-day period, the same decan was visible on the horizon, and during the hours of darkness the time was calculated by the position of a given constellation at a specific point in the sky.

Two calendars were used by the Egyptians who, although fully aware that the solar year was $365\frac{1}{4}$ days in length, employed a calendar for official records and dating consisting of 365 days without inserting an intercalary day in any year to make up the deficiency, as is done with the Leap Year in our present calendar. The result was that the opening day of the year worked back through the solar year until a whole cycle had been completed after a period of 1,460 years. This "sliding" year was divided into three seasons of four months, each of thirty days, to which were added five epagomenal or intercalary days devoted to festivals of the five principal deities, when all business activities were suspended. The months, subdivided into three periods of ten days, and grouped into fours, gave three seasons: "the season of inundation" (spring), "the season of emergence" (winter), presumably signifying the reappearance of the land from the receding flood waters; and "summer", written with a word which could imply "drought" or "deficiency of water". Events were dated as occurring, for example, in "Year 4 of King So-and-So, third month of Inundation, day 7".

In order to organize the opening day of the year to coincide with the annual celestial events of the solar year, and to follow the seasons at the proper times, the so-called "Sothic" calendar was operated which was defined as beginning with the heliacal rising of the Dog Star Sirius (or Sothis, as it was called by the Greeks) at a time when it is seen on the horizon just before sunrise. This, with very little variation, marked the first day of the seasonal year, and a sixth day was intercalated, normally every fourth year, in addition to the five epagomenal days of the "sliding" year, in order to keep the two in relation to one another. The dates of certain important events were sometimes recorded at the time of a heliacal rising of Sirius, thus enabling these dates to be pin-pointed in accordance with our own chronological system and other dates to be calculated within the preceding and following astronomical cycles. There are therefore one or two dates in Egyptian history of which there can be absolute certainty, but, unfortunately, these instances are so few that long periods must be approximately dated by deductions from archaeological and textual evidence.

The Julian calendar of 45 B.C. was based on the Egyptians' solar year of $365\frac{1}{4}$ days and originally placed the first day of January five days after the winter solstice, while the five epagomenal days were scattered throughout the year; it is the saints' day calendar of the Christian churches that preserves more clearly the traces of the old Egyptian calendar. The slight variation in the Sothic calendar led finally to the confusion of calendars which existed at the Roman epoch; and the same difficulty arose when Pope Gregory in 1582 introduced our present calendar and which he tried to overcome by attempting to fit a calendar to the tropical year.

The calendars the Egyptians used were intelligent and neat, and had the advantage over our own of avoiding unequal months, and the overlapping of weeks with months and years.

By the end of the sixth century B.C. the knowledge and skill of the Egyptian doctors and physicians were acknowledged throughout the Near East, and there is little doubt that early Greek medicine owed much of its theory and practice to the Egyptians, particularly in the realm of nature and animal drugs and their application. For example, the virtues of colocynth, coriander and alum had long been recognized by the Egyptians, as well as those of hartshorn and tortoiseshell; while castor oil and honey had also long been used by them in the treatment of gastric disorders and for throat and respiratory complaints.

Medicine in Egypt can be said to have been well established during the Old Kingdom, if not before, and although the earliest known medical papyri date from the Middle Kingdom it is fairly obvious that they were based on material of a much earlier date. The names of many Old Kingdom physicians are known, and Imhotep, Djoser's architect, traditionally acquired fame as a skilled physician. His temple at Memphis became in the Ptolemaic period a centre for pilgrims coming to seek cures at his shrine. Here he was worshipped as a god, while the shrine was also a centre for the study of medicine, being visited by Greek medical students, and thus enhanced the reputation of the Egyptian doctors and physicians in the Mediterranean world, to whom Hippocrates and Galen, to name only two, acknowledged their indebtedness.

Much of the medical texts remains obscure, owing to the difficulty in translating and identifying correctly the names of diseases, parts of the body, and the drugs and other instruments of treatment; but the general conclusion seems to be that methods of diagnosis and treatment were largely empirical and based on practical observation. Nevertheless, they were inextricably mixed with magic, since illness and injury were often deemed to be caused by malevolent spirits who inhabited the chaotic world outside the limits of ordered creation. Consequently magic formed a large part of the treatment prescribed, and took the form of spells and incantations recited over amulets and statuettes which were given to the patient to wear, and which were also worn constantly as a protection against physical and other ills. That they materially helped in the cure is more than likely inasmuch as they created in the patient a state of mind and perhaps a degree of relaxation which directly affected some complaints. Many revolting concoctions were swallowed by the patient in order to eject the evil spirit: animal fat and dung were used in the mixtures, and instances occur of dead mice being given to sick children. These have actually been found in the mummified bodies of children, probably given in a last effort to save their lives. Many of these recipes found their way into Greek and medieval *materia medica* and thence to the west, and some were still employed in backward parts of Europe and even in England and America in our own era.

The Egyptians suffered as much then as they do now from various forms of eye diseases, and from earliest times efficacious treatments were used, including the application of kohl to the eyes for protection against the sun and insects. The modern treatment of hemeralopy, or night blindness, with liver extract was also known, in a crude form, to the Egyptian doctors who advocated that "liver of ox roasted and crushed out be given against it. Really excellent!"

Many medical notes and treatises have been found describing the symptoms and treatment of eye complaints and gynaecological conditions and diseases specially relating to childbirth, which survive in the Greek and medieval medical works, where they seem to have directly derived from Egypt. Knowledge of anatomy, however, was surprisingly limited, considering that the practice of mummification must have familiarized them with the existence and location of many internal organs – they did, in fact, have names for all the external parts of the body – but the process used probably prevented very accurate observation. It did, however, create the necessary conditions for future vivisection and experiment at a time when in neighbouring countries the cutting up of the human body after death was forbidden or was precluded by the custom of cremation.

In the field of bone surgery they were fairly advanced in diagnosing and setting fractures and dislocations, but there is little or no evidence of the performance of any major surgical operations. Splints were made of wood padded with linen, and it is thought that wounds were closed with surgical stitching and dressed with linen swabs and bandages.

One surgical papyrus contains a systematic list of injuries and case histories, each one being classified under its title: a statement of the condition to be treated; the examination: "If you examine a man having a wound in his head, you should say concerning him: 'an ailment not to be treated' or 'this is an ailment I will treat', or 'try to treat' ". Then follows the nature of the treatment to be given, and finally the prognosis: "This man will live".

Dentistry was also practised, and teeth were extracted, probably with an iron implement, while dental fillings of some mineral cement were used for "fastening a tooth"; filled teeth, sometimes bound with gold, have actually been found in the heads of mummies.

The Egyptians kept annals of important historical events occurring in the reigns of their kings, but historical records consisted mainly in the compilation of lists of royal names and the length of regnal years. The reign of each king was counted from year one, so that in dating historical events in Egyptian history recourse must be had to

other methods. Apart from these annals and lists, happenings were recorded, if at all, in the form of stories and admonitions attributed to various historical figures and kings, though often written long after their lifetime. To satisfy their curiosity about the past, or to point the moral for the present and future, the Egyptians relied on these stories and popular legends of bygone events.

In the sphere of geography, Egypt was thought of as the centre of the world, and while they possessed sufficient knowledge of neighbouring countries and of navigation to reach them, and certainly showed an adventurous spirit when it came to exploring new territories, they had only the vaguest idea of their geographical situation or of the shape of the world. They orientated themselves by the Nile so that to "sail downstream" meant to go northwards, and the word was written with the sign of a boat without sails, oars being sufficient, to progress downstream with the current. "To sail upstream" meant to go southwards against the current, and was written with a boat in full sail filled with the north wind from the Mediterranean. When foreign conquests took them to the Euphrates, which flows from north to south, they laughed in derision at a river which flowed "upside down".

A people who lived on, and by the produce of, the Nile were naturally born sailors from time immemorial, and as well as being complete masters of navigation up and down the Nile, which presented no very great difficulties, they were experienced sea-farers and navigators of the Mediterranean and Red Sea coasts, and there exists a tradition that a voyage of exploration was made round Africa.

Pictures of boats appear on predynastic pottery, and in pharaonic times a steady shipbuilding industry was carried on in the royal dockyards. Boats and ships of all sizes were made, from reed skiffs to large wooden ships with decks and cabins, propelled by two rows of oars and by one or two sails secured by yards. Steering was controlled by a pilot in the stern with one or two large oars. Large fleets of warships were built in later times for conveying troops overseas and to combat pirates from the Aegean who, in Ramessid times, became an increasing menace to the peace of Egypt. Several accounts of battles with "the Peoples of the Sea" are recorded with graphic illustrations on the walls of temples of this period.

The Nile was the main highway of Egypt, and cargo boats constantly fared up and down the river conveying corn, cattle, vegetable produce and commodities of all kinds, including the building materials and obelisks for pyramids and temples. River trans-port and navigation were organized with the usual Egyptian efficiency and control, and a large section of the population provided a permanent body of experienced sailors and seamen. The popular stories did not neglect this typical aspect of life and include tales of shipwrecked sailors and voyages to foreign lands.

The Nile also provided the last journey for the dead, whose funeral processions of boats carrying the mummy followed by a fleet of mourners and funeral furniture and equipment must have formed one of the most impressive and colourful sights of the unending panorama which the Nile traffic must have presented at all times.

The Egyptians have left a large quantity of nautical terms and of drawings and models for ships, which retained much the same form until modernized by the Greeks and Phoenicians.

Top left. Ship with sails and oarsmen; carved relief from the tomb of Ti. Old Kingdom. *Left*. Wooden model of a boat

Chapter Twelve

ARTS AND CRAFTS

The foundations of Egyptian art were laid in predynastic times in the manufacture of objects of everyday use. The symbolic significance attached to every human action by a primitive people was reflected in the objects which served the necessities of life, every aspect of which was imbued with magic. When, with the development of a stable society, civilization in its true sense began, and men had leisure to direct their thoughts and energies beyond the basic needs of existence, these objects became the vehicles for expressing more spiritual aspirations and ideas beyond their purely practical use and so assumed ornamental or ceremonial forms. For example, the predynastic palettes which were used for mixing eye-paint came to be used for ceremonial purposes and as historical documents, like the palette of Narmer. The designs on these palettes imbued as they were with meaning, became the traditional way of representing outstanding historical events and gave rise to permanent motifs in future artistic representation.

The typical forms of architecture which are seen throughout Egypt in temples and monuments of all periods had their beginnings in the utilitarian bricks made from Nile mud, and in the tree trunks and bundles of reeds and rushes bound together to make primitive dwellings and shrines, later to be copied in stone and developed into the impressive papyrus and lotus columns of Luxor and Karnak. These forms, developed and firmly established by about 2800 B.C., became crystallized by virtue of the sanctity attached to their original purpose for housing the primitive gods and remained as part of the cult necessary to maintain the "right order".

The Egyptians paid the price of their conservatism in endeavouring by outward forms to guarantee the stability of their world. The art and architecture of the Old Kingdom are characterized by a sincerity of spontaneous effort and creative delight inspired by unquestioning faith; and this is never recaptured by later generations. Its forms were to be faithfully and rigidly copied over and over again, with some variations and accretions, it is true, but basically they remained the same, and while later works may indeed show an advance in technique and confidence they never again expressed the youthful spontaneity and integrity of the Old Kingdom. There were periods of degeneration and vulgarity interspersed with periods of resurgence, and, later still, a conscious archaic revival when the most beautiful work was produced, modelled on the Old Kingdom masterpieces, but the fact that these renaissance artists were deliberately conscious of the significance of what they were doing gives the impression of creation by rote without the sincere striving for perfection born of the urge to materialize deeply felt beliefs.

The Amarna breakaway from artistic tradition under Akhenaten's influence was so un-Egyptian – and, in any case, was such an esoteric form of art – that it hardly affected the country as a whole. On the other hand, there is no doubt that although the philosophy which inspired it did not survive, its repercussions in later artistic forms are perhaps due to the fact that relaxation of tradition brought to a head with artificial suddenness a trend that was already apparent in an artistically gifted people confined by the rigid conventions imposed upon them by their beliefs.

Although no artist's name has ever been found on a work of art, and no paintings are ever signed, there is little doubt that artists were highly esteemed members of the community. They were men of great talent and intellect, particularly those working in the temples and tombs, and must have had to acquaint themselves with the liturgy and mythology of the scenes they were called upon to portray, and to be familiar with the contents of the religious texts and literature. One artist says of himself that he "knew the divine words and the conduct of festivals", and the complicated names, titles and protocol of the gods and royal personages had to be inscribed without error. They were conscious of their own worth, like one who described himself as "an artist that excels in his art, a man above the common herd in knowledge". Tomb-owners were happy to pay tribute to the sculptors and painters they employed, and it is evident that they were well rewarded for their skill; the special position of the Deir el-Medina workmen and artists speaks for itself. It was a rich man's boast that he employed a well-known artist for his tomb, "no mere copyist", he says, "but one who made the inscriptions with his own hands, whose inspiration comes from his heart . . . a scribe of dexterous fingers and of good understanding in all things".

The temples, whose imposing ruins in Middle and Upper Egypt, at Karnak and Luxor and in Nubia, impress the visitor not only by their size and architectural construction but by their peculiarly satisfying aesthetic proportions, nearly all date from the New Kingdom and the Late Period. Nevertheless it is known that they embody in their basically uniform plan the traditional elements of the cult of the god's house in spite of local variations and additions acquired over the course of centuries.

The ground plan, construction, and design of the temple evolved with the cult to include all its aspects and ritual, and the hardest stone was used as the material offering the most permanent stability that could be found. In building, endowing and restoring the temples, the king was fulfilling his proper function in maintaining the stability of the world, and the daily rites performed in them in his name by his delegated priests was an essential part in reconciling the all-powerful gods, whose agent he was, to act on his behalf. In this sense, a temple was more the economic centre of the community than the religious centre of the people's worship, comparable perhaps to a central electricity power station in our own time on which the whole population depends but whose mysteries and working are left to the professional experts to carry out, in which the public plays no part and to which access is forbidden. The Egyptian people had no access to the temples except at special seasonal festivals, such as the harvest, or the coronation of a new king, and then only to the outer precincts, when the god was brought out of his sanctuary and carried in procession on a sacred bark by the priests in accordance with special rituals performed by the king.

Each constituent part of the temple represented a cosmic element in the life of the land, from the plants and vegetation carved on the base of the walls representing the earth and its crops, to the stars and flying birds painted on the ceilings, the symbolic

The entrance to the temple of Horus at Edfu

roof of the world. The huge halls of columns combined the architectural function of supporting the roof with symbolic representation of the sacred groves of trees or papyrus thickets originally surrounding the primitive shrines. Every part of the temple and every scene depicted on its walls held some ritual and cultural meaning, and the whole edifice stood for a microcosm of an ordered universe. It was by virtue of the magic inherent in material creation that life was guaranteed. This significant intention was embodied in every aspect of the building of the temple, from its inception and choice of site by the personal inspiration of the king, to its planning, orientation, foundations and actual construction and decoration; and each stage was accompanied by appropriate ceremonial. In pursuing this ideal, the Egyptian architects and builders through their adaptive genius solved the technical problems involved in erecting these magnificent structures, and, by accident as it were, created thereby forms which, in their grandeur and harmony, are unique in pre-classical architecture. They evoke a strangely vivid and gratifying response in the beholder by their proportions and symmetry, at the same time leaving a baffling sense of incomprehension as regards the inner significance of their oddities and peculiarities of structure and decoration. Apart from any other consideration, it remains a mystery how these monuments, so impressive still in their majestic ruins, were built without any mechanical aid save a few primitive measuring instruments, stone, copper, or bronze implements, and human labour, however unlimited and thoroughly well organized the latter might be.

The general plan of an Egyptian temple is typified by those of the New Kingdom, and, though modifications and variations occur, the central part remained constant.

Left. The court and vestibule of the temple of Horus at Edfu. *Right.* Approach from the hypostyle hall to the sanctuary in the temple of Horus at Edfu

The entrance was gained through large double doors of pine overlaid with bronze or gold (none of these doors have survived), set between two pylons, or stone towers covered with scenes carved in relief, to the faces of which were fixed long flag-poles, attached by wooden or stone sockets, from which fluttered coloured banners of the king and the gods. The pylons were topped with a cavetto cornice, a typical and universal feature of Egyptian architecture, derived from the prehistoric prototype of reeds tied at their tops with a horizontal band. Next came the forecourt, open to the sky, and surrounded by a covered colonnade. Steps led from this court into the hypostyle or pillared hall, running along the temple axis, the columns supporting the roof, the central ones being sometimes higher than the rest to form clerestory openings for light and ventilation. This in turn led to the sanctuary where the statue of the god was kept in a granite shrine. Surrounding the sanctuary were often grouped smaller shrines dedicated to related gods and goddesses, and a series of chambers associated with the sanctuary served for vestries, sacristies and storerooms. The approach to the holy of holies, which began in the brilliant sunshine of the open outer court, became increasingly dim through the hypostyle hall, and all the way a lowering of the roof level and a slight raising of the floor increased the sense of mystery and awe in the approach to the sanctuary where total darkness prevailed. The only temple where this sensation can be appreciated now is the Ptolemaic temple of Horus at Edfu, which retains its roof.

Even the vast complexity of temples and pylons at Karnak where, from the Middle Kingdom onwards, successive kings added their own temples, courts and pylons in every direction, adheres basically to this plan.

Every part of the walls, columns and pylons was covered with inscriptions and reliefs, all placed according to ritual, and every temple had attached to it a sacred lake, the whole enclosure being surrounded by a girdle wall of mud-brick, itself also covered with scenes and inscriptions.

Leading out of the first court was the entrance to the king's palace where he resided when carrying out temple ceremonies, and the remaining foundations of some of these palaces indicate that their layout was a smaller version of the temple with the throne-room as the focus of the building.

The forms of the shrines which housed the god retained in stone right through the Dynastic and Late Periods the archaic forms of those of the predynastic gods of Upper and Lower Egypt, the former being little more than a reed tent, the latter a kind of kiosk with a hoop-shaped roof with a reed parapet, the prototype of the later cavetto cornice. These primitive shrines are known only from the hieroglyphic signs with which they were written.

The winged disk, so commonly seen adorning the lintels of doorways and cornices, is an ancient emblematic form of the sun-god Rē, flanked by cobras, the forms of two ancient goddesses of Upper and Lower Egypt, combined with the wings of the falcon-god Horus, and is a typical example of the Egyptians' happy facility in combining several symbolic features into a symmetrical and pleasing design, in this case one which spread throughout the Mediterranean world and into Europe.

The original supporting columns of palm trunks or bundles of reeds tied together had been reproduced in stone by the Third Dynasty, as seen in the engaged stone columns of Djoser's buildings at Saqqara.

They were the forerunners of the free-standing columns already perfected by the Fourth and Fifth Dynasties. From this time onwards buildings were supported by columns of two main types, the square-sectioned monolithic column from which were developed fluted columns when the four angles were cut off, followed by the octagonal, when four more angles were cut, the final stage being the sixteen-sided column. The facets of these columns are as often flat as they are concave, so that to call them "proto-Doric", as has been done, is something of a misnomer. The Greek Doric column has a distinct taper towards the top, while the Egyptian column is straight; and while the Greek column has a large overhanging capital made from a separate block, the Egyptian capital is often flush with the block above it.

The papyrus column has a circular shaft, often with a fine ridge running longitudinally at intervals round it in imitation of the shape of the reed; it tapers slightly at the base where it was often carved and painted to represent pointed leaves. The shaft diminishes as it ascends, and several horizontal lines round the top of the shaft just below the capital imitate the bands of reeds which originally tied the papyrus bundles together. The capital was carved to represent papyrus umbels, either tied together or with open heads. In later times the shaft lost its fine modelling and became merely the background for inscriptions and decoration in colour, as exemplified by those in the Ramessid temples when a vulgar degeneration into sheer bulk replaces the graceful columns of earlier periods.

The lotus column does not taper at its base, and the ridged line does not occur on the shaft. The capital imitates several lotus buds, or open flowers, tied together. Smaller

122

Left. Papyrus column of pink granite in the chapel of Tuthmosis III at Luxor temple. *Right.* Columns in the hypostyle hall, Karnak temple

lotus buds are inserted downwards through the binding lines below the capital representing the branch which tied them together.

The palm column is chiefly known from the Old Kingdom and the Late Period. It resembled the trunk of the palm tree, and the capital was carved to imitate the upright fronds of the palm.

The use of columns in temples suggested the form of the mummified Osiris, and a much favoured type of column was the Osiris pillar, the face being carved to represent the king. Fine examples are the Osirid columns which adorned the terraces of the temple of Hatshepsut at Deir el-Bahri, in this case the carved features representing the queen. Another favourite type was the Hathor column, the capital being formed with the head of this female cow-goddess, with human face and cow's ears, the whole pillar representing a sistrum, her particular symbol.

In the New Kingdom columns were elaborately inscribed and brightly painted, and the effect in a hypostyle hall such as that of Karnak must have been magnificent in the extreme.

The roofs which the columns supported were made of heavy slabs of stone, generally flat, although other forms of roofing were employed such as the corbelled roof, a series of tiers of stone slabs or bricks, each course projecting beyond the previous one as they rose until they met at the top, and "false arches", made by setting two granite blocks at an angle in a socket cut into the blocks on which they rested.

The approach to many temples was guarded by a double row of sphinxes. The lion was traditionally the guardian of sacred places, and by virtue of its invincible attributes the lion's body was given a human head representing the sun-god or the king, the connection between the two being obvious. The sphinxes of the famous avenue leading to the temple of Amūn at Karnak are carved with rams' heads, this animal being associated with Amūn. The Egyptians called the sphinx "living statue", the name sphinx having been given by the Greeks, who confused it with the winged woman-headed lioness of their own mythology whose enigmatic and evil characteristics were quite different from those of the lion of Egypt, and it is extremely doubtful whether the Greek sphinx owes its derivation to Egypt.

The Egyptians' extraordinary skill in low and sunk relief sculpture attained its highest degree of perfection in the earliest dynasties, to judge by the reliefs in Djoser's pyramid and the private tombs of the Old Kingdom, and in the few remaining temple reliefs of that period (plate 7).

After the surface to be carved had been dressed it was squared up by vertical and horizontal lines made by faint incisions, or by stretching string dipped in red ochre and lightly touching the surface of the walls with it. The design, for which a small scale model or plan had previously been prepared on papyrus by the master artist, was sketched on the walls by the draughtsmen in red or black paint. It was then incised in raised or sunk relief, and details of the design were modelled on the relief. The soft limestone at Giza and Saqqara provided an ideal surface for the delicate shallow relief found in the tombs and temples there. The scribes took charge of the accompanying texts, and were followed by the painters who coloured the reliefs. Every surface of the wall and ceiling was completely covered with carvings and inscriptions.

A strict convention was adhered to in depicting the human figure, with the head in profile, the eye in what amounted to a front view, the shoulders shown frontally, the chest with a three-quarter view, and the legs and feet in profile. Although a few experiments in perspective were essayed, the general view was always two-dimensional. This, with the strange convention attached to the human figure, creates at first sight an odd effect, though once it has become familiar, the strict proportions, fluent lines, symmetrical composition and fine detail exercise a charm and satisfaction of their own. For sheer technical virtuosity, Egyptian relief work has seldom been equalled and never successfully copied. In admiring the quality of these reliefs and of surviving sculpture in the round it is sometimes forgotten that the great majority were originally entirely covered by brightly coloured paint – which has only rarely withstood the lapse of time – so much so that it must have obscured many of the finer details of the modelling which are now visible.

The Egyptians' love of colour led them to paint everything: walls, statues, reliefs and small objects of all kinds. It had become the custom at the beginning of the New Kingdom to replace relief sculpture in the tombs by painted scenes, owing partly to the spread of tomb-ownership among a wider section of the population who could probably afford neither the time nor expense involved in the execution of relief work, and partly to the emergence of the technique of tempera at this period.

The pigments used were naturally-occurring minerals, or artificially prepared mineral substances, which were finely ground on stone palettes and mixed with water to

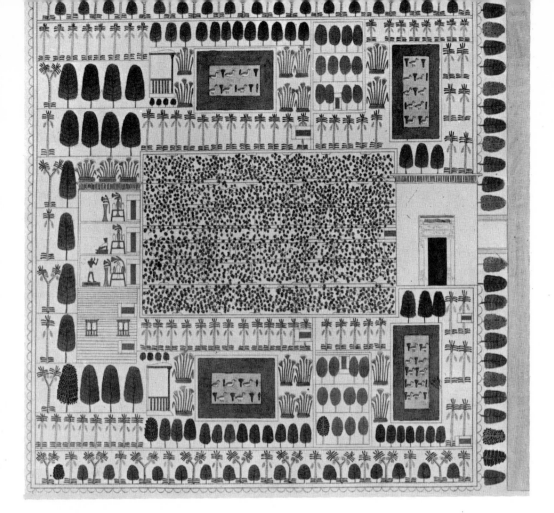

Painting of a house and garden, from a Theban tomb

which gum or glue was added as an adhesive. The scribes used the same method for writing material, writing on papyrus being a form of painting. Black was obtained from carbon soot or powdered charcoal; azurite or a crystalline compound frit was used for blue; and malachite (a copper ore), or a similar frit, was used for green. Red and yellow were commonly red and yellow ochres, or red iron oxide and yellow orpiment, and white gypsum was used for whiting. For large surfaces a brush of fibrous wood or palm fibre was used, the tip being frayed out by soaking in water, while finer work was done with a single stem of rush with a frayed end like the scribes' rush pens.

In limestone areas the walls had a good natural surface to take the paint, but when the quality of the rock was poor it had first to be dressed and the irregularities filled up with mud plaster. Over this was applied a coat of plaster which was covered with a pale coloured wash as a background for the design. For applying the wash a short brush of halfa grass or palm fibre, rather like a shaving brush, was used, and the same method for marking out the design was used as for relief work.

In drawing or painting there was no more attention paid to perspective than in relief sculpture, and a house and garden were drawn flat. If a pool was shown sur-

Left. Slate statue of King Menkaurē and his queen (Dyn. IV). *Centre.* King Amenemhet III (Dyn. XII). *Right.* Grey granite statue of the Lady Sennuwy, wife of a royal prince who was governor of Asyut (Dyn. XII)

rounded by trees, the trees would be drawn flat. A box and its contents, which would not normally be visible, were drawn by superimposing the contents on the picture of the box itself; a house was shown with its interior and occupants, presumably on the grounds that what was known to be actually present must be included in the picture, whether or not it was visible.

Colour was applied quite flat, but some attempts at shading are found in New Kingdom work. In painting birds, flowers and vegetation the details were brought out with great delicacy and skill, demonstrating a remarkable aptitude for observation and feeling for the subject.

It was a convention that men should usually be coloured red-brown and women yellow, while Nubians were shown black, and great attention was given to portraying racial characteristics of the features and costume of these and other foreigners, the artist being more free from rigid rules when depicting nature, or ordinary people who did not participate in the privileges of those whose status allowed them the right of a decorated tomb. The tomb-owner and his wife, and figures of the king and important dignitaries, were always drawn on a larger scale than the rest of the surrounding scene.

Conventions in statues and statue groups remained basically those laid down in the Old Kingdom, but style and workmanship varied in each period so that it is possible to assess the date of the majority of pieces.

In the Old Kingdom the view was frontal, the position standing or seated. Kings always stood with the left foot advanced, or were seated on a block representing the throne, and the effect was one of static nobility with no impression of movement. Great care was bestowed on the head and features, the rest of the body being treated quite casually. A pillar was attached to the back for support and for the accompanying inscriptions. The features of the king were idealized to emphasize his divine nature, and private individuals of the nobility adopted a similar pose and style.

Head of King Sesostris III of the Twelfth Dynasty

The Middle Kingdom sculptors showed more human traits in the features of their rulers, who were characterized by thoughtful and sometimes careworn expressions, pointing to a more humanizing aspect of the monarchy. Tomb models, which appear first in the Middle Kingdom, allowed freer representation of ordinary people, but private statuary continued to follow the royal style.

The New Kingdom was the period of statues of monumental proportions, and while conventional idealism persisted there was a tendency towards portraiture, and individual likenesses are easily traced.

In creating a statue, the sculptor used a block of limestone, granite, diorite or other hard stone roughly resembling the desired shape and size. After sketching the design in red ochre and roughly blocking out the shape, details and features were modelled with copper and bronze chisels, or, when working with the hardest stone, by pounding with a round dolerite pounder, chipping with stone chisels, and rubbing vigorously with stones of various sizes aided by an abrasive, probably quartz-sand. The finishing touches were made entirely by eye, with patient light burnishing. Finally the statue was polished and almost invariably painted.

The Nineteenth Dynasty excelled in colossi like the enormous statues of Ramesses II, notably those in his temple, the Ramesseum at Thebes and at Abu Simbel in Nubia.

Quality and style varied at different periods in spite of the strictly held traditions which, with the exception of the Amarna period, remained fairly constant, and it is possible to distinguish between different workshops, and between work of the best master craftsmen and the varying grades of workmanship from the provinces. There were periods of decline in standards – notably in times of political unrest – and of revival, and a definite decline occurred in the colossal sculpture of the late New Kingdom when size and bombast seemed to be the most important criterion. In the renaissance period of the Twenty-Sixth Saite Dynasty, the Old Kingdom classical forms and styles were

127

admired and consciously copied with a return to simple pure lines in posture, dress, and technique, but although it produced some beautiful work comparable with the old models, it lacks their spontaneous exuberance and calm assurance and shows traces of fussiness and at times effete self-consciousness. The best of these late examples, however, can easily be mistaken for Old Kingdom work, but, like most revivals and copies, in spite of the skill and good taste which they display they lack something of the integrity and pure simplicity of the originals from which they were copied.

The large body of craftsmen engaged on producing the utensils and luxuries with which Egypt abounded are lost in oblivion as individuals, but are immortalized by the large amount of their handiwork which still survives to adorn museums and collections throughout the world, and by their representation as personalities in their own right by their fellow-craftsmen, the painters and sculptors, in many a scene showing them at work in the workshops of potters, jewellers, carpenters and metal foundries.

The earliest craft of all was that of the potter, and the best pottery was made in predynastic times. The polished red and black ware was modelled by hand before the invention of the potter's wheel in the Fourth Dynasty. In the dynastic period the quality of the pottery declined, although in the New Kingdom very attractive painted pottery of a reddish colour was made, decorated with flower and other motifs influenced by Asiatic and Cretan designs. Similarly the manufacture of stone vessels of all shapes and sizes, and fashioned from the hardest stones, reach a perfection and harmony in shape and finish during the first three dynasties that was never surpassed and seldom equalled in subsequent periods. Later, more malleable materials such as serpentine and alabaster were used for the more elaborately shaped vessels of the Middle and New Kingdoms which, during the New Kingdom, were subject to influences from the Mediterranean and Mesopotamia. The large ornate alabaster vessels which became fashionable during the Eighteenth and Nineteenth Dynasties, and are exemplified by those found in Tutankhamūn's tomb, show an exuberance of fantastic detail and ornamentation that can only be marvelled at for the execrable taste they display. Less offensive are the ornate lamps made of alabaster and painted with coloured designs which glowed brightly when lit from the inside. A commoner form of lighting was by means of earthenware dishes placed on raised supports of carved wood, and shaped like branches of papyrus, on the flowers of which the little dishes were fixed by metal bands. Oil was used for burning, the wick being made of twisted strands of linen.

The Egyptians' love and keen observation of plant and animal life was exemplified in the New Kingdom products; some of the small luxury articles such as toilet spoons and jars, and other purely ornamental objects made in the forms of birds and animals, possess a delicate and imaginative charm.

Egyptian glass was opaque and brightly coloured, the method of blowing not being introduced into Egypt until Roman times. It was not generally made, save sporadically, until the New Kingdom when it was used for making beads, vases, and objets d'art and as inlay for furniture and jewellery.

The most prolific survivals of small objects from Egypt are the attractively brilliant beads, amulets, vases and tiles, and other small objects which were manufactured in innumerable quantities from the Middle Kingdom onwards. The material from which they were made is known as Egyptian faience, which is not the same as the true faience, but an alkaline glazed quartz frit of a sandy composition held together by natron. The glaze has a distinctive shade of green or blue ranging from the palest turquoise to the deepest indigo. Faience was used as a substitute for semi-precious stones and also for larger objects such as bowls, statuettes (plate 1), and other vessels. It was also used for making seals and scarabs, but the origin of these typically Egyptian objects, which first became prolific during the First Intermediate period, goes much further back to the time when a reed or small pebble with distinctive markings was first used to impress a lump of damp clay so as to identify ownership of private property. These patterns were developed into conventional designs to which were added the owner's name and titles. The reed became the cylinder seal, and pebbles were transformed into stamp or button seals.

The man who first made an impression with his signet on a lump of plastic clay started a process which had far-flung consequences: he had discovered the principle of printing, and doors were sealed with clay and stamped before locks and keys were invented. The Mistress of the House was in charge of the household stores, and seals have been found buried with women in their tombs. The housewife's string of seals has become the modern housekeeper's bunch of keys, and a man gave his wife his seal as a sign that she was mistress of his possessions and in charge of the household stores. Worn at first on a string of beads round the neck or wrist, and later secured by string or wire to the finger, the modern counterpart of the seal is the wedding ring.

Seals made in the form of the scarabeus beetle, which had magical connotations in Egyptian mythology, became common in the Middle Kingdom and were used throughout Egyptian history. Scarabs were also popular as charms and amulets with mottoes and spells inscribed on them. They were pierced with holes, strung on thread, and worn tied to the garments or on the finger. They were made from many kinds of materials, steatite, stone and faience, and some have been found made from semi-precious stones and of gold. Large inscribed scarabs were issued by some pharaohs to commemorate notable events, such as a royal marriage; and a series of scarabs of Amenhotpe III of the Eighteenth Dynasty appeared celebrating a decade of successful lion-hunts in which the king played a prominent part: "Statement of lions which His Majesty brought down with his own arrows from the year 1 to the year 10: fierce lions, 102."

A large scarab was placed on the heart of the mummy and, being the symbol of re-birth, was inscribed with a prayer that the heart might not betray its owner when being weighed in the balance of Truth in the judgment before Osiris.

Many semi-precious stones were mined in Egypt, including carnelian, jasper, felspar and amethyst, as well as the prized turquoise from Sinai, and lapis lazuli from Afghanistan which was imported through Mesopotamia. These stones were fashioned with the greatest ingenuity and imagination by the jewellers and set in gold or other metal alloys, and the utmost variety of patterns and designs was obtained by stringing the various types of semi-precious or faience beads into broad collars or necklaces. The jeweller's art reached its finest peak in the Middle Kingdom, the jewellery of the royal princesses found at Dahshur and Lahun being among the finest ever found; while specimens found in the tomb of Tutankhamūn demonstrate the wealth and magnificence of the New Kingdom pharaohs, especially when it is remembered that Tutankhamūn was far from being the greatest of them all. The tomb robbers of ancient times

130

Top right. Tutankhamūn's heart scarab (*left*); and Middle Kingdom jewellery, made of gold and lapis lazuli, found at Dahshur. *Right*. A bead collar found in the tomb of Tutankhamūn. The beads are made of faience coloured yellow, red, green, blue, and white, with a clasp in the form of a lotus flower

have no doubt seen more splendid treasure still which will never now be recovered.

Gold came from the native mines of the eastern and south-eastern deserts, and from Nubia. The precious metal was a monopoly of the State like everything else, and was kept in the temple treasuries and issued in rings and bars and carefully weighed before being handed over to the goldsmiths for working. They, and the other metal-workers, formed part of the personnel of masons, sculptors, carpenters and jewellers attached to the temple workshops, permanently employed in producing the gifts of all kinds which the king dedicated to the gods or distributed among the priests and courtiers and other state servants in payment or as largesse for services rendered.

Gold was highly prized not primarily for its monetary value, since money and coinage were unknown and it was only in the New Kingdom that certain gold weights were used to evaluate quantities of payments for goods in kind. It was valued for its intrinsic beauty and qualities of endurance. Its gleam was equated with the life-giving rays of the sun, and yellow was consequently a specially venerated colour. The use of gold for the adornment of the king's person, alive or dead, for statues of the gods and for tomb furniture and equipment (plate 13), was intended rather for its eternal life-giving properties than for its value as treasure in our sense of the word. The divine properties of gold conferred survival, and it was called "the flesh of the gods". When its material value became apparent from the eagerness of her neighbours to procure it, Egypt turned this to account by trying to gain a monopoly of gold, and it formed an important part of the tribute levied from foreign dependencies and from Nubia, and was diplomatically used in trade and other political transactions with the heads of neighbouring states.

Silver, which until the Middle Kingdom was more highly prized than gold, was not obtainable in Egypt and had to be imported from Syria and the Aegean. It was worked with the same degree of skill as gold, and was called "the white metal" and said to be "the bones of the gods". A remarkable find at Tanis in the Delta in 1940 brought to light the tombs of some rather obscure kings of the Twenty-first and Twenty-second Dynasties and some of their officials in which the coffins, vessels, facial masks and other appurtenances were of engraved silver, the workmanship being of the highest order. This horde makes a magnificent display in the Cairo Egyptian Museum.

The Egyptian carpenters achieved a high degree of workmanship in ornamental carving on furniture (plate 14) and other articles of domestic use, which they made from native trees, employing joinery and true mortices, secured by wooden tenons and metal or gold-studded nails. The tools used were copper or bronze axes, saws, chisels, adzes and drills. Furniture and boxes were inlaid with semi-precious stones, ivory, ebony and glass, and the richest furniture was often overlaid with gold and silver leaf.

Wood from Lebanon was used for sarcophagi and for ships and masts as well as for structural and other purposes for which more serviceable wood was required than that provided by the native trees.

Plate 15. A scribe of the Fifth Dynasty. This painted statue was found at Giza in 1951 in a tomb near the Great Pyramid, and is a fine example of Old Kingdom sculpture
Overleaf Plate 16. Weighing the heart of the deceased in the judgment hall of Osiris

Chapter Thirteen

MUSIC AND MUSICIANS

There is plenty of evidence to show that, as with most oriental peoples, music and dancing played a prominent part in the religious and secular lives of the Egyptians, but while the instruments they played are known there are no clues as to how their music sounded, nor have any certain examples of notation been found, so that it is not even known whether it was in fact written down or was improvised in the usual manner of folk music. It is reasonable to suppose that the ritual music and dances performed in the temple ceremonies followed a set liturgical form, and probably conformed to a standard pattern so that some means of learning the music and steps to be performed, whether by rote or by written notation, must have been devised. There were directors of music in charge of the choirs and bands permanently attached to temples and palaces, and wives and daughters of the priests and nobles took part in the ritual dances before the gods, and in processions at special festivals when they performed slow rhythmic dances to the accompaniment of the sistrum, which they carried in their hands and shook in time with their steps. The small metal hoop, shaped like a horseshoe, was strung with wires and mounted on a handle carved with the head of the goddess Hathor who was generally depicted holding a sistrum which was associated with her. Across the wires were threaded small metal discs which, when shaken, produced a soft clear sound. The sistrum must be one of the oldest musical instruments in the world which is still in use. It was known in Egypt from the very earliest times, and is still used today in the services of the Coptic Church.

Among the titles of ladies is found that of "Songstress of Amūn"; and a "Director of Royal Song" records in his tomb that he and his choir "rejoiced the heart of His Majesty by our song".

No Egyptian party or banquet was complete without music and dancing which were provided by professional men and women musicians and young dancing girls. The singers accompanied themselves on the lute or harp, or sang in concert accompanied by an orchestra of harps, oboes, lyres and single and double flutes, while others sat on the ground beating time by clapping their hands. Dancing girls were dressed in the scantiest of costumes, their hair attractively arranged in curls on either side of the face or in two or three long tresses. In the period of the Old Kingdom the orchestras were formed entirely of men, and women only played the harp, but in the New Kingdom men's and women's voices were blended, especially in the ritual songs sung in the temples, and orchestras were mixed. Harpists were then often male, and were generally depicted as being blind. During the same period, percussion instruments were added, small drums, tambourines and castanets being introduced from Asia together with the lyre and zither and the lute. Probably the oldest instrument of them all, and one which

Plate 17. Egyptian pottery, *Upper left:* veined limestone jar (predynastic, before 3100 B.C.); *upper right:* banded calcite bowl (protodynastic, before 3100 B.C.); *lower left:* two anhydrite ("blue marble") cosmetic pots held by monkeys carved in low relief (Dyn. XII); *lower right:* serpentine cosmetic pot (Middle Kingdom)

Military trumpet of silver embellished with gold, the bowl shaped like a lotus flower, with a protective wooden core which fits inside the trumpet, probably to protect it in transit. From the tomb of Tutankhamūn

originated in Egypt, was the flute, made of reeds and wood and with a mouthpiece of papyrus. There were short flutes, blown horizontally, and long ones played vertically like a recorder. Another importation from Asia was the trumpet, which was used chiefly for military purposes for signalling and issuing orders. Of the three trumpets found in the tomb of Tutankhamūn, one was made of copper and two of silver ornamented with gold, the bowl end shaped like the calix of a lotus flower. On the copper trumpet was inscribed a dedication to "the Legions of Rē, Amūn, and Ptah". These trumpets have actually been played with a modern mouthpiece and produced a high-pitched somewhat melancholy sound, unless this impression was the result of hearing their call breaking a silence of more than three thousand years.

The Egyptians enjoyed above all else entertaining their friends to a banquet, when the main reception hall of the house would be gaily decorated with lots of flowers and garlands of foliage. Small stands and tables would be laden with joints of meat, game, and duck, with dishes of fruit, cakes and sweets. Wine flowed freely, and both men and women drank their fill and more.

The guests were received by the children of the house and the servants, who escorted them to their host and hostess who stood in their columned hall to receive them, exchanging fulsome compliments all the way. They sat in pairs on low chairs or stools and were served by young maidens and youths who, having presented each guest with a lotus and hung a garland of flowers around his neck, then proceeded to hand round cups of wine and sweetmeats. The food was eaten with the fingers, and small alabaster finger-bowls and a linen towel were also handed round to each guest.

Good manners were observed by the guests in not looking too interestedly at the food and drink provided, and by refraining from overt comment on what was offered. It was the duty of the host to provide the best he could within his means in order to "gain the praises of god, and a good reputation among men". When the feast was well under way, and the dancers and musicians and acrobats had entertained the guests, a more relaxed mood prevailed in which a blind harpist's song might find a receptive and sympathetic audience to listen to his philosophic reflections, which were perhaps only acceptable in an atmosphere engendered by plenty of good food and drink and congenial company.

Painted scene of a banquet, from the tomb of Nakht, an official and priest of Amūn (Dyn. XVIII)

The burden of his song seems to strip away all the comforting safeguards erected by accepted beliefs, which must have been questioned by the more thoughtful among the intelligentsia in the advanced stage of civilization that had been reached at the time of its composition. The poet in effect counsels his hearers to "enjoy this happy day so long as you are able, for one day each man and woman that is born must go to his or her appointed place. . . . Pass the day therefore in happiness." He refers to what has befallen the tombs of the ancestors, their walls being in ruins, their habitations no more. He flatters the host by telling him that it will not be thus with him: "The walls of your house are secure: you have planted sycamore trees on the margin of your pool, and your spirit rests beneath them and drinks of their moisture. Follow your heart's bidding and falter not while you are on earth. Give bread to him that hath no possessions, that your repute may stand high forever." Then, striking a more cynical note, "Pass the day in happiness. . . . Think on the day when you must fare to the land where all men are as one. Never did any man take his possessions with him to that land, and none can thence return."

This does not seem to tally with the beliefs and funerary customs by which the Egyptians set so much store, but what society, when it has advanced from its origins to a highly educated and sophisticated level, does not belie its declared beliefs by its practice in daily life? Or it may be just another instance of the Egyptians' adaptability in accepting all sides of a question as true, however contradictory, and the harpist's desire to please his audience by justifying and encouraging their merriment.

To point the moral further, the harpist sang about the fate of the pyramids and tombs of former kings, the violation and neglect of whose monuments over the centuries must have been obvious to all, and goes on: "The gods who were of olden time and who rest in their pyramids, likewise the mummies and the spirits buried deep in their pyramids . . . their places are no more . . . their sanctuaries are destroyed as though they had never been, and none comes to tell what manner of men they were, or of their possessions. While yet you live, therefore, follow your heart's desire and your happiness as long as you are on earth . . ."

BIBLIOGRAPHY

Aldred, Cyril. *The Development of Egyptian Art*. Alec Tiranti, London, 1962

Aldred, Cyril. *The Egyptians*. Ancient Peoples and Places series, Thames and Hudson, London, 1961

Černý, Jaroslav. *Ancient Egyptian Religion*. Hutchinson's University Library, London, 1952

Edwards, I. E. S. *The Pyramids of Egypt*. Rev. ed., Penguin Books, 1961

Frankfort, H. *Ancient Egyptian Religion, An Interpretation*. Columbia University Press, New York, 1949

Gardiner, Sir Alan. *Egypt of the Pharaohs*. Oxford University Press, London, 1961

Harris, J. R. *Egyptian Art*. Spring Books, London, 1966

Introductory Guide to the Egyptian Collections in the British Museum. British Museum publication, London, 1964

Kees, Hermann. *Ancient Egypt*. Trans. Ian F. D. Morrow. Faber, London, 1961

Lange, K., and Hirmer, M. *Egyptian Architecture, Sculpture, Painting in 3000 Years*. Phaidon Press, London, 1956

Montet, Pierre. *Everyday Life in Egypt in the days of Ramesses the Great*. Trans. A. R. Maxwell-Hyslop and Margaret S. Drower. Arnold, London, 1958

Posener, Prof. Georges (ed.). *A Dictionary of Egyptian Civilisation*. Trans. Alix MacFarlane. Methuen, London, 1962

ACKNOWLEDGEMENTS

Plates 1 and 17 and the illustration on page 82 are reproduced from photographs (© George Rainbird Ltd 1968) taken especially for this book by Derrick Witty in the Department of Antiquities in the Ashmolean Museum, Oxford, by kind permission of the Keeper. Plates 12, 13 and 14 are reproduced from photographs by F. L. Kenett (© George Rainbird Ltd 1963).

For permission to reproduce copyright illustrations, grateful acknowledgements are made to:

Alinari: page 88 *right*

Ashmolean Museum, Oxford, Department of Antiquities: pages 88 *left*, 90 *centre left* and *bottom*, 102 *top right* and *bottom*; Griffith Institute: pages 26 *left*, 29, 30, 43 *top*, 84, 85, 131 *top left* and *bottom*, 138

British Museum: plates 9, 16; pages 43 *bottom*, 48 *right*, 68 *right*, 76 *left*, 89, 90 *centre right*, 92 *left*, 93 *right*, 104 *centre* and *bottom*, 127

Camera Press: page 128

J. Allan Cash: pages 51, 56 *bottom*, 74 *left*, 123 *right*

H. Rolf Gardiner: page 104 *top*

Hirmer Verlag: pages 14 *bottom*, 28, 32, 46 *left* and *right*, 47, 48 *left*, 75 *top left, top right* and *bottom*, 92 *right*, 102 *top left*, 126 *centre*, 139

A. F. Kersting: pages 57 *top*, 74 *right*, 120, 121 *left* and *right*

William MacQuitty: page 76 *right*

A. Mekhitarian, Fondation Égyptologique Reine Élisabeth, Brussels: plate 2; pages 14 *top*, 15, 20, 23, 64 *bottom*, 66, 93 *left*, 111, 116 *top*, 123 *left*, 131 *top right*, endpapers

Metropolitan Museum of Art, New York: 26 *right*, 61 *top*, 68 *left*, 116 *bottom*

Musée du Louvre: plate 8; pages 33 *left* and *right*, 94

Museo Egizio, Turin: page 21

Museum of Fine Arts, Boston: pages 61 *bottom*, 64 *top*, 126 *left* and *right*

Office du Livre, Fribourg, Switzerland: pages 38, 56 *top*

Oriental Institute, University of Chicago, Illinois: plates 3, 4, 5, 11; pages 24, 25, 57 *bottom*, 77, 81, 87, 90 *top*

The Trustees, Sir John Soane's Museum, London: page 42

Roger Wood: plates 6, 7, 10, 15; page 41

The maps on page 11 were drawn by Joan Hardman

INDEX

The page numbers in *italic type* indicate illustrations

Abu Simbel, 73, 127, *76*, *128*
Abydos, 39, 40, plate 7
Abyssinia, 16
Achaemenides, 19
Adultery, punishments for, 87, 109
Aegean Sea, 65, 117, 132
After-life, afterworld, *see* Death and after-life
Agriculture, *see* Farming
Ahmes-Nofretiri, Queen, 81
Akhenaten, 70, 73, 83, 91, 118, *75*
Alabaster, 16, 41, 129, *20*, *42*, *43*
Alexander the Great, 10, 12
Alexandria, 12, 112
Amarna, 67, 70, 79, 83, 91, 118, 127
Amenemhet I, 59, 60; III, *126*
Amenhotpe I, 81
Amenhotpe III, 67, 91, 130
Amon-rē, 67, 70
Amosis I, 65, 67; ceremonial battle axe of, *64*
Amulets, 62, 129, 130
Amūn, 27, 29, 65, 70, 73, 77, 78, 87, 108, 110, 124, 137, 138
Anatomy, knowledge of, 115
Ani, plate 16
Animal worship, 10, 87-8
Anthropomorphic deities, 10
Anubis, 24, 108
Arabian desert, 13
Architecture, *see* Houses and villas, Palaces, Pyramids, Temples, Tombs
Armour, 65
Army, 63, 65-6, 77
Arsinoë, 20
Asklepios, 46
Assyrians, 12, 67, 77
Astronomy, 113
Aswan, 10, 13, 69
Aten, 70, 73

Babylonians, 112
Baḥr Yûsuf, Lake, 20
Beads, 129, *131*
Bedjmes, 49, *48*
Beer, 88
Bes, *84*, *85*
Birds, 27
Board games, 89, 91, *90*
"Book of the Dead", 62, 108, plate 16

Bouza, 88
Burial practices, *see* Death and after-life, Tombs
Byblos, 38

Cairo, 13, 45
Calendars, 113-14
Cambyses, 12
Canals and dykes, 19, 20, 21
Canopic jars, 44, *43*
Canopus, 44
Carpentry, 132
Carter, Howard, 73
Cats, 87, *88*, *90*, plates 5, 11
Cattle, 27-8
Cavetto cornice, 121, 122, *74*
Cedar oil, 42, 44
Champollion, Jean François, 103, 105
Chariotry, 65
Cheops, *see* Khufu
Children's dress, 93; games, 91; toys, 91, *90*
Cleanliness, household, 85; personal, 84-5
Cleopatra, 105
"Cleopatra's Needle", 69
Clepsydra, 113
Climate, 22
Coffins, 40, 41, 47, 62, 132, *61*, plate 12
Colossal statues, 73, 127, *128*
Columns, 118, 120, 122, 123, *56*, *123*, plates 6, 10
Cooking methods, 22, 89
Coptic language, 103, 106
Coptos, 60
"Corn Osiris", figures, 39
Cosmetic pots, spoons, 129, *93*, *94*, plate 17
Cosmetics, 94
Crocodile, 20, 91
Crocodilopolis, 20
Crops, 22
Cuneiform script, 67
Cylinder seals, 130

Dahshur, 130, *131*
Dancing, 137
Death and after-life, 10, 31-44
Death penalty, 109-10
Defacing of tombs, 37

Deir el-Bahri, 110; temple of Hatshepsut, 69, 70, 123, *74*
Deir el-Medina, 80-1, 83, 119, *82*
Delta region, 10, 11, 12, 13, 15, 27, 29, 38, 63, 132
Demotic script, 103
Den, *76*
Dendera, *38*
Dentistry, 115
Deserts, 15, 23-4, 63
Diodorus, 42
Diplomacy, 66, 80
Divorce, 87
Djoser, King, 46, 49, 52, 106, 114, 122, 124, *48*, plates 6, 10
Dogs, 88
Domestication of animals, 27-8
Domestic life in Egypt, 83-94
Donkey, 19, 28
Dress, 12, 92-3, *92*
Duamutef, *43*
Dykes, *see* Canals and dykes

Early Dynastic Period, 10
Ebony inlay, 84, 132
Edfu, 27, 121, *120*, *121*
Education, 95-6
Eighteenth dynasty, 63, 67, 81, 129, 130
El-Baharîya, 15
Electrum, 69
Eleventh Dynasty, 59
El-Farâfra, 15
El-Qurna, 110
Embalming, 34
Embroidery, 89
Empire, *see* New Kingdom
Entertaining, 138-9, *139*
Epitaphs, 107
Ethiopia, 13, 65
Euphrates river, 10, 65, 67, 70, 117
Eye, diseases of the, 115
Eye make-up, 94
Exports from Egypt, 80

Faience, 41, 129-30, *131*, plates 1, 12
Faiyûm, 20, 59, 62
Falcon, falcon god, 27, 58, 122. *See also* Horus
"False doors" in tombs, 40, *41*
Farming, 55, 70

Fifth Dynasty, 38, 122
First Cataract, 10, 13, 60, *14*
First Dynasty, 16, 45
First Intermediate Period, 109, 130
Fish, fishing, 19, 20, 25, 91
Floors, painted, 83
Flowers, Egyptian love of, 25-6
Food, 88
"Food of Egypt" vineyard, 30
Footwear, 93
Forced labour, 110
Fourth Cataract, 65
Fourth Dynasty, 47, 49, 122, 129
Fowling, 91, plate 11
Furniture, 83, 84, 92, 129, 132, *84 85*

Galen, 114
Game, 24
Games, 89, 91, *90*
Gardens, 85, *125*
Geometry, 112
Giza, 46, 47, 50-2, 124, *51, 56*
Glass, 129; inlay, 83, 129, 132, plate 12
Gold, gold-work, 60, 67, 83, 84, 132, *66, 131*, plates 12, 13
Great Green, The, 13, 15
Greece, Greeks, 9, 20

Hair styles, 12, 92, 93
Hapy, 16, *43*
Harems, 86
Hatshepsut, Queen, 67, 69-70, *68*; temple of, Deir el-Bahri, 69, 70, 123, *74*
Hathor, 137, plate 7; Hathor column, 123
Heliopolis, 55, 69, 70, 108
Heracleopolis, 59
Herodotus, 13, 42
Hesirē, tomb of, *102*
Hieratic script, 103, 106, *30, 104*
Hieroglyphic script, 15, 55, 62, 77, 101, 122, *76, 104*, plate 14; decipherment of, 9, 103, 105-6
Hippocrates, 114
Hippopotamus, 25, 91, *25*
Historical records, 115, 117
Hittites, 67, 70, 73, 77
Homer, 11
Horemheb, 73
Horoscopes, importance of, 113
Horse-breeding, 65
Horus, 27, 38, 55, 58, 122; temple of, Edfu, 121, *120, 121*
"House of Life", 55, 95
Houses and villas, 83-4, *125*
Hunting, 19, 20, 24, 91
Hyksos, 63, 65, 67, 89
Hypostyle, 73, 121, *123*

Imhotep, 46, 106, 114
Imsety, *43*

Incense, 27
Inlay, 83, 84, 129, 132. *See also* Ebony, Glass, Ivory
Intermediate Period, 10
Isis, 39, 40, plate 7
Ivory casket, plate 14; label, *76*; inlay, 84, 132

Jewellery, 62, 92, 129, 130, *131*
Julian calendar, 114
Justice, 109-10

ka, 34, 40
ka-priests, 34, 37
ka-statue, 37
Kadesh, battle of, 77-8
Karnak, 67, 69, 73, 76, 118, 119, 121, 123, 124, *75, 123*
Kawit, Sarcophagus of, *92*
Khafrē, King, 50, 52, *56*
Khârga-Dâkhla, 15
Khnumhotep, tomb of, *23*
Khufu, 50, 52, *51, 56*
Kohl, 94, 115

Lahun, 130
Lapis lazuli, 130, *131*
Late Period, 10, 49, 87, 119, 122, 123
Law and Justice, 109-10
Lebanese wood, 132
Libyan desert, 13, 20; kings, 12
Lighting, forms of, 129
Lion, 124
Lisht, 60,
Literature 55, 101, 106
Lotus, 26, *14, 131, 138*; Lotus column, 26, 83, 122
Lower Egypt, 10, 13, 22, 29, 45, 63, 69, 122
Lustration rites, 38
Luxor, 11, 19, 37, 67, 77, 118, 119, *74, 123*

"Maat", 31, 107, 108
Magic used in treatment of illness, 114-15
Malkata, 91
Manners, importance of, 95, 138
Market-gardening, 22
Marriage, 86-7
Masks, 132
Mastaba tombs, 39, 45, 47, 52, 62
Medicine, 114-15
Medinet Habu, 73, 76
Mediterranean Sea, 13, 22, 117
Meketrē, tomb of, Thebes, *61*
Memphis, 16, 45, 52, 114, *20*
Menes, 16, 45
Menkaurē, 50, *126*
Menna, tomb of, *57*
Mentuhotpe II, 59
Mercenaries, 65
Mereruka, tomb of, Saqqara, 40, 50, *25, 41, 81*

Mesopotamia, 38, 129, 130
Middle Egypt, 10, 11, 13, 20, 67, 119
Middle Kingdom, 10, 11, 27, 59-62, 63, 87, 101, 114, 127, 129, 132
Mines, mining, 49, 63
Mitanni, 67
Morality and ethics, 107-8
Mud-bricks, 83, 118, 122
Mummification, 16, 31, 34, 42, 44, 115, *111*, plate 8
Mural painting, *see* Painting
Music, musical instruments, 137-9, *138, 139*
Mut, 27

Nakht, *139*, plate 5
Narmer, King, 45; Palette of, 45, 118, *46*
Natron, 16, 42, 85
Naucratis, 12
Nebamun, tomb of, plate 11
Nefertiti, 70, *75*
Nefertum, 26
Nekhbet, 27
Neset, *33*
Neskhons, Canopic jars of, *43*
New Kingdom, 10, 11, 16, 19, 23, 29, 40, 42, 49, 63-78, 80, 83, 87, 91, 92, 106, 110, 119, 120, 123, 126, 127, 129, 130, 132
Nile, Nile Valley, 10, 13, 15, 16, 19-21, 22, 39, 45, 60, 69, 108, 110, 117, *14*
Nile goose, 87
Nineteenth Dynasty, 44, 129
Nomes, Nomarchs, 47, 52, 59
Nubia, 10, 11, 13, 49, 52, 60, 63, 88, 117, 127, 132
Numerical system, 112

Oases, 15, 29, 63
Obelisks, 69, *74*
Oils, 22-3, 27
Old Kingdom, 10, 11, 12, 34, 37, 38, 39, 45-58, 60, 63, 69, 87, 91, 92, 93, 106, 114, 118, 123, 124, 126, 127, 129, 137
Olive oil, 23
Orontes river, 77, 78
Osiris, 27, 38, 39, 40, 44, 58, 108, 130, *38, 128*, plate 8; Osiris pillar, 123
Ostraca, 81, 82, 106, *82*

Painting, 224-6; in houses, 83, 92; on pottery, 129; on sculpture, 124, *82, 85, 88*, plates 9, 15; in tombs, 31, 59, 62, 124, *21, 23, 24, 26, 29, 57, 61, 90, 125, 139*, plates 2, 3, 4, 5, 11
Palace architecture, 91-2
"Palace façade" pattern, 47, *47*
Palestine, 23, 65, 66, 67, 70, 73
Palette of Narmer, 45, 118, *46*

143

Palm column, 123
Papyrus, 101, *104*, plate 16; papyrus
    column, 13, 83, 122, *123*, plates
    6, 10; papyrus plant, 13, 15, 22,
    23, 25, *14*, *97*, plates 3, 5
Pelusium, 30
Peneb, 81
Peoples of the Sea, 73, 117
Pepi II, 52
Perfumes, 26–7
Persians, 77
Pets, 87–8
Ploughing, 55, *89*
Plume of War, 65
Portrait-statues, 31, 40, 49, *33*
Postal system, 60
Pottery, 129, plate 17
Priesthood, 55
Ptah, 16, 65, 77, 78, 138
Ptolemaic kings, 10, 12, 114
Ptolemy V, 103
Ptolemy Lagus, 12
Punt, land of, 27, 69
Pylons, 121, *74*
Pyramids, 33, 37, 112; at Lisht, 60;
    at Giza, 46, 47, 50–2, *51*, *56*; at
    Saqqara, 46–7, 49, plate 10
Pyramid texts, 55, *57*

Qebhsenuef, *43*
Quarrying, 49

Rainfall, 22
Ramesses II, 29, 76, 77, 110, 127,
    76, *128*
Ramesses III, 73, 76, *77*
Ramesses IX, 110
Ramesseum, Thebes, 73, 77, 82,
    127
Ramessid period, 73, 122
Rē, 26, 37, 38, 55, 65, 77, 108, 122,
    138
Red Crown of Lower Egypt, 45, *14*,
    46
Red Sea, 27, 117
Reed plant symbol, 13
Relief sculpture, *see* Sculpture
Reptiles in desert, 24
Ritual music, dances, 137
Roman Empire, 10
Rosetta Stone, 103, 105, *104*
Royal Scribe, rank of, 66, 81

Sahara desert, 13
Sais, 12
Saite period, 12, 127
Saqqara, 37, 45–7, 49, 50, 122, 124,
    25, *28*, *32*, *41*, plate 6, 10
Sarcophagi, 40, 41, 47, 60, 132, *42*,
    47, *92*
Scarab, 130, *131*
Scientific knowledge, 112–17
Scribes, 55, 58, 65–6, 96, 101, plates
    15, 16; equipment of, 96, 101, *102*

Sculpture, 52, 62, 126–7, 129; relief
    carving, 31, 65, 69, 119, 122, 124,
    25, *28*, *32*, *38*, *43*, *46*, *47*, *76*, *81*,
    84, *85*, *87*, *92*, *116*, plates 7, 17;
    statues, 49, 73, 127, *26*, *33*, *48*,
    68, *75*, *88*, *102*, *126*, *127*, *128*,
    plates 1, 9, 15. *See also* Wood
    carving
Seals, 130
Second Cataract, 60
Semi-precious stones, 130, 132, *131*
Semitic tribes, 63
Senenmut, 69, *68*
Sennuwy, Lady, *126*
Sepa, *33*
Serdab, 39, 49
Serpentine, 129, plate 17
Servants and retainers, 89
Sesostris, *14*, *127*
Seth, 38, 39, 58, 63, 65, 77, 78
Sety I, 41, 110, *42*, *111*; temple of
    Abydos, plate 7
Shabti statuettes, 21, plate 1
Shadûf, 19, 85, *21*
Sheep, 27, 28
Shipbuilding, ships, 49, 117, 132,
    116
Shrines, 47, 121, 122
Silver, silver-work, 83, 132, *138*
Sinai peninsula, 49, 52, 130
Sistrum, 123, 137, plate 7
Siwa, 15
Sixth Dynasty, 40, 52
Slavery, 80
Sobek, 20
Society, structure of, 79–82
Sorghum, 22
"Sothic" calendar, 113
Sphinx, 16, 52, 124, *20*, *56*
Steatite, 130
Stelae, 34, 40, 76
Step Pyramid, Saqqara, *see* Pyra-
    mids
Stone age culture, 15
Stone vessels, 129, plate 17
Sudan, 13, 88
Sundials, 113
Swamps, 19, 23, 25
Syria, 23, 66, 67, 73, 132

Tanis, 132
Tapestry weaving, 89
Taxation, 80
Temples, 33, 49, 52, 55, 58, 62, 65,
    67, 69–70, 118, 119–24, *56*, *74*,
    120, *121*,
Tetisheri, Queen, plate 9
Thebes, 11, 27, 59, 63, 69, 70, 73,
    77, 80, 108, *21*, *26*, *61*, *87*, plate 3
Third Cataract, 60
Third Dynasty, 46, 47, 49, 60, 122
Thoth, 108, *102*
Throwstick, 25, *91*
Ti, tomb of, Saqqara, *28*, *32*, *116*

Tiles, 49, 129
Toilet preparations, 93–4, *93*
Tomb robberies, 32, 110
Tombs, 31, 37, 39–41, 70; offerings,
    34, 39, *61*; painting, 31, 37, 59,
    62, *21*, *23*, *24*, *26*, *29*, *57*, *61*, *90*,
    125, *139*, plates 2, 3, 4, 5, 11;
    relief carving, 31, 37, 40, 124, *15*,
    25, *26*, *28*, *32*, *41*, *81*, *87*, *116*
Toys, 91, *90*
Trade with other countries, 60, 63,
    80
Trees, 23, 85
Turquoise, 130
Tutankhamūn, 73; tomb of, 15, 26,
    40–1, 44, 89, 92, 129, 130, 138, *24*,
    26, *30*, *43*, *84*, *85*, *138*, plates 12,
    13, 14
Tuthmosis I, 65, 67, 69
Tuthmosis III, 69, 70, 110, *75*
Twelfth Dynasty, 11, 60
Twentieth Dynasty, 73
Twenty-first Dynasty, 110, 132
Twenty-second Dynasty, 132
Two Lands, 10

Unas, 55
Underworld, 31, 41, 55
"Upholder of Egypt" vineyard, 29
Upper Egypt, 10, 13, 29, 45, 63, 69,
    119, 122
Userhet, tomb of, plate 4

Valley of the Kings, 41, 80
Vegetables, 22
Vegetation gods, 39, plate 8
Villages, 83
Vines, vineyards, 28–30, plate 2
Vizier, office of, 49–50, 79, 81, 109
Vulture, 27; Vulture head-dress,
    27, plates 7, 9

Wadi Natrûn, 16
Wadis, 15
War, Egyptian attitude to, 76
Water wheel, 19
Wax cones, scented, 27, *26*
Weapons, 63, *64*
Weaving and spinning, 89
"Weighing of the heart", 108, plate
    16
White Crown of Upper Egypt, 45,
    14, *46*
White Walls, 45
Wigs, 93, *92*
Wild life, 24–5, 62
Wines, *see* Vines, vineyards
Winged disk motif, 122, *14*
Wisdom Texts, 106
Women's status in the home, 86
Wood-carving, 62, *61*, 89, *92*, *94*,
    102, *116*

Young, Dr Thomas, 103